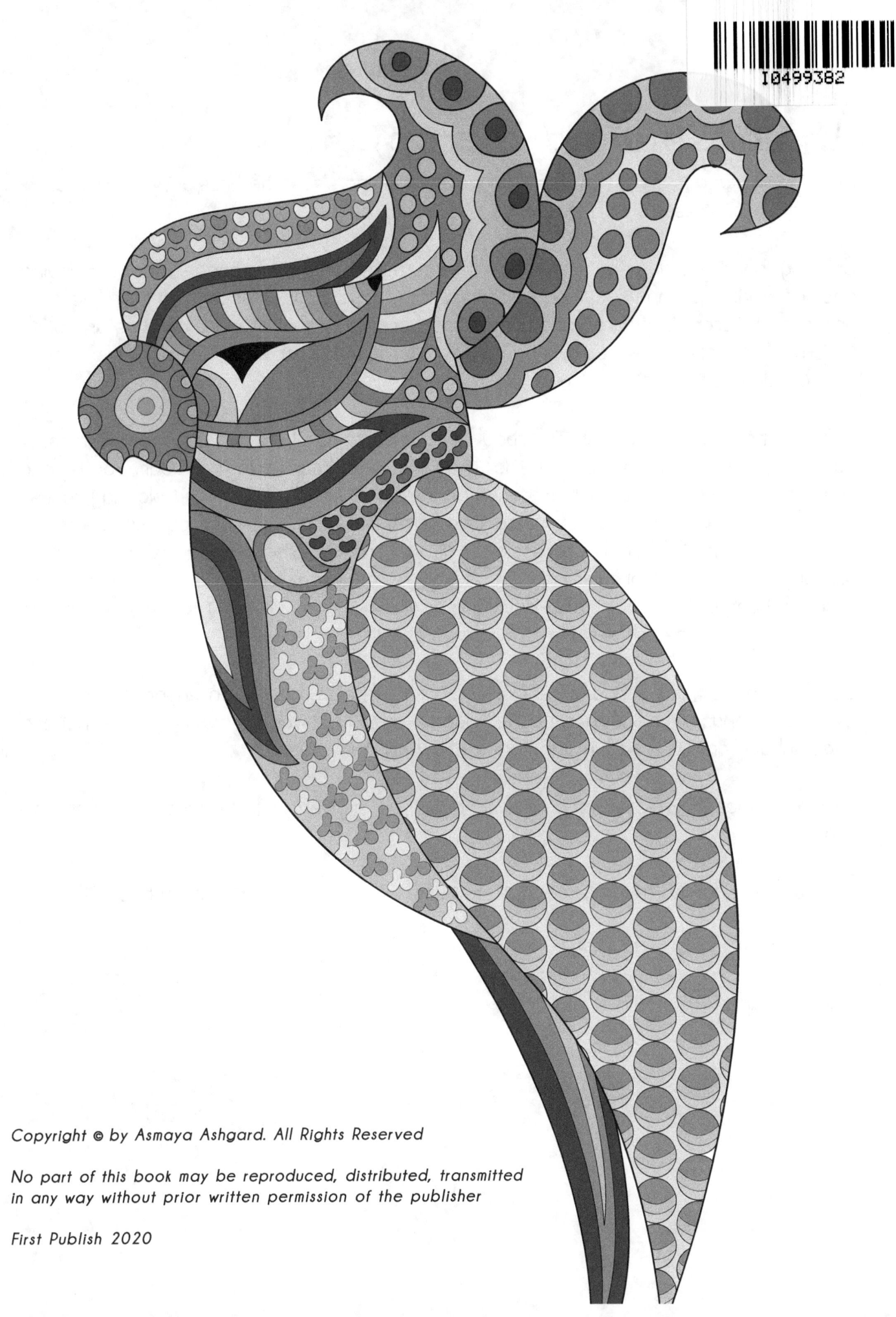

Copyright © by Asmaya Ashgard. All Rights Reserved

No part of this book may be reproduced, distributed, transmitted in any way without prior written permission of the publisher

First Publish 2020

About Coloring Therapy

Coloring therapy is an essential medium for relieving stress and restoring calm in a busy, chaotic, stressful world like ours.

Coloring therapy is done by using one's energy and thoughts to concentrate and bringing back one's attention and focus on Coloring within the lines and concentrating on the process. Different colours bring out different emotions and it can be used as an outlet to remove negative energies and built up emotions in the form of Coloring. It is almost an alternative to meditation if done right.

Coloring therapy or meditation isn't about being thoughtless. I fact it is about being mindful, yet being able to let go of all the thoughts and keep bringing your focus and attention back to your breath (like in case of meditation) or back to your Coloring process (like in case of Coloring therapy) According to the American Art Therapy Association, art therapy is a mental health profession in which the process of making and creating artwork is used to "explore feelings, reconcile emotional conflicts, foster self-awareness, manage behavior and addictions, develop social skills, improve reality orientation, reduce anxiety and increase self-esteem.

Coloring therapy has a added benefit of making one bring out something creative into the world along with being therapeutic. It has an added satisfaction of creating something beautiful and artistic. This will bring out the lost artist in you.

Like Pablo Picasso said every child is an artist, the problem is remaining one when you grow up.

So bring out your artist and let go of the stress with this Coloring therapy book.

Happy Coloring :)

COLOR TEST PAGE

YOU CAN SKETCH ANYTHING HERE

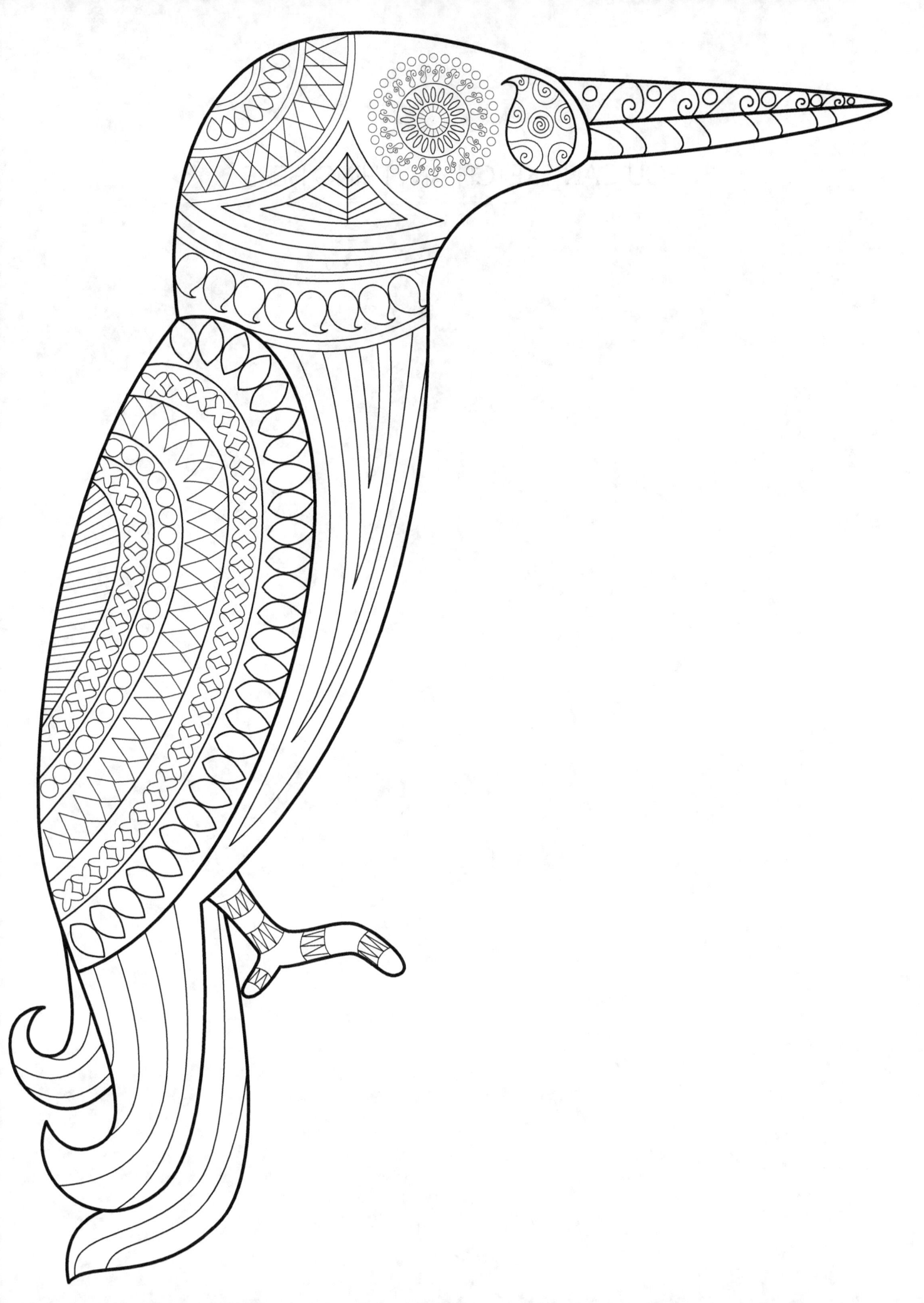

YOU CAN SKETCH ANYTHING HERE

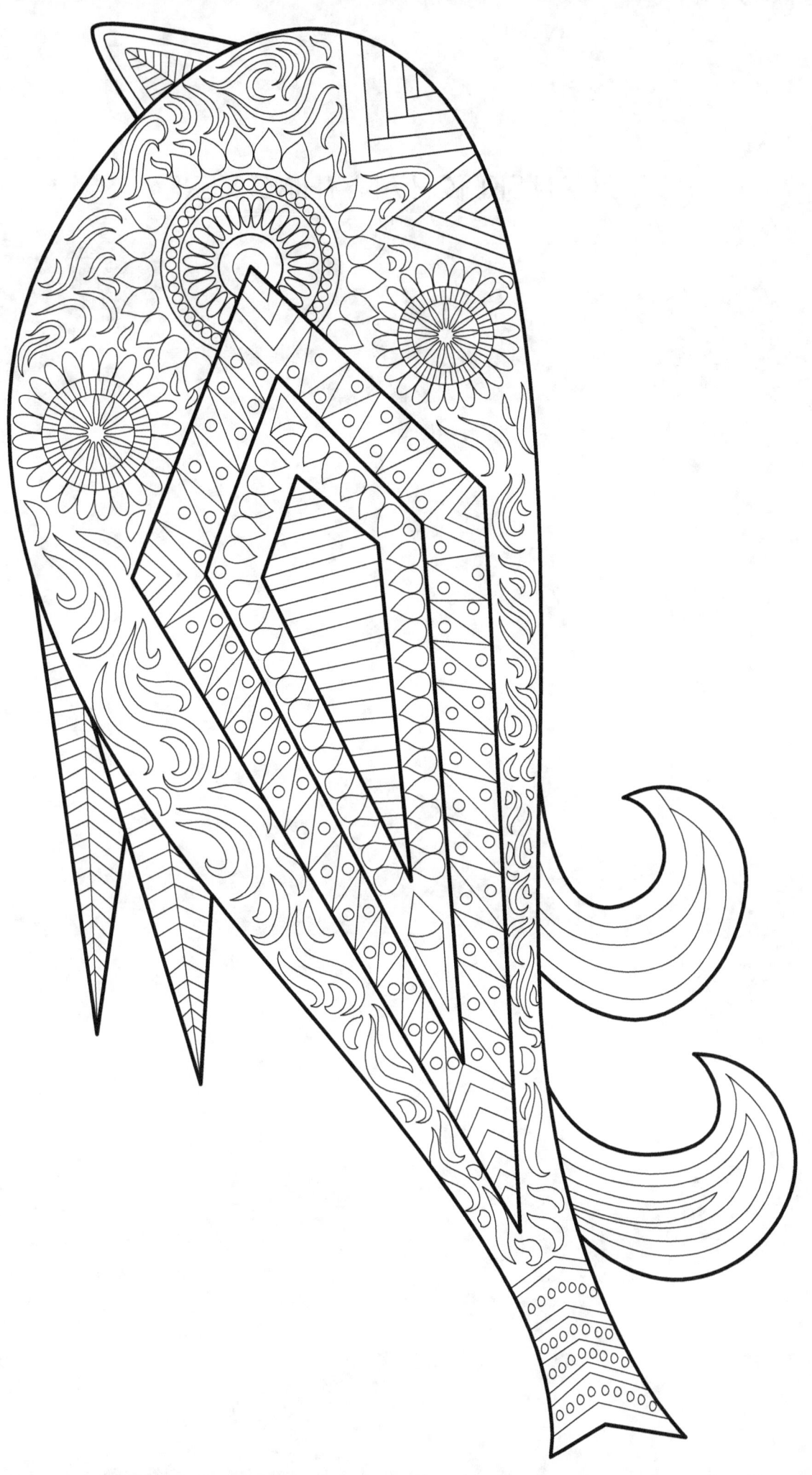

YOU CAN SKETCH ANYTHING HERE

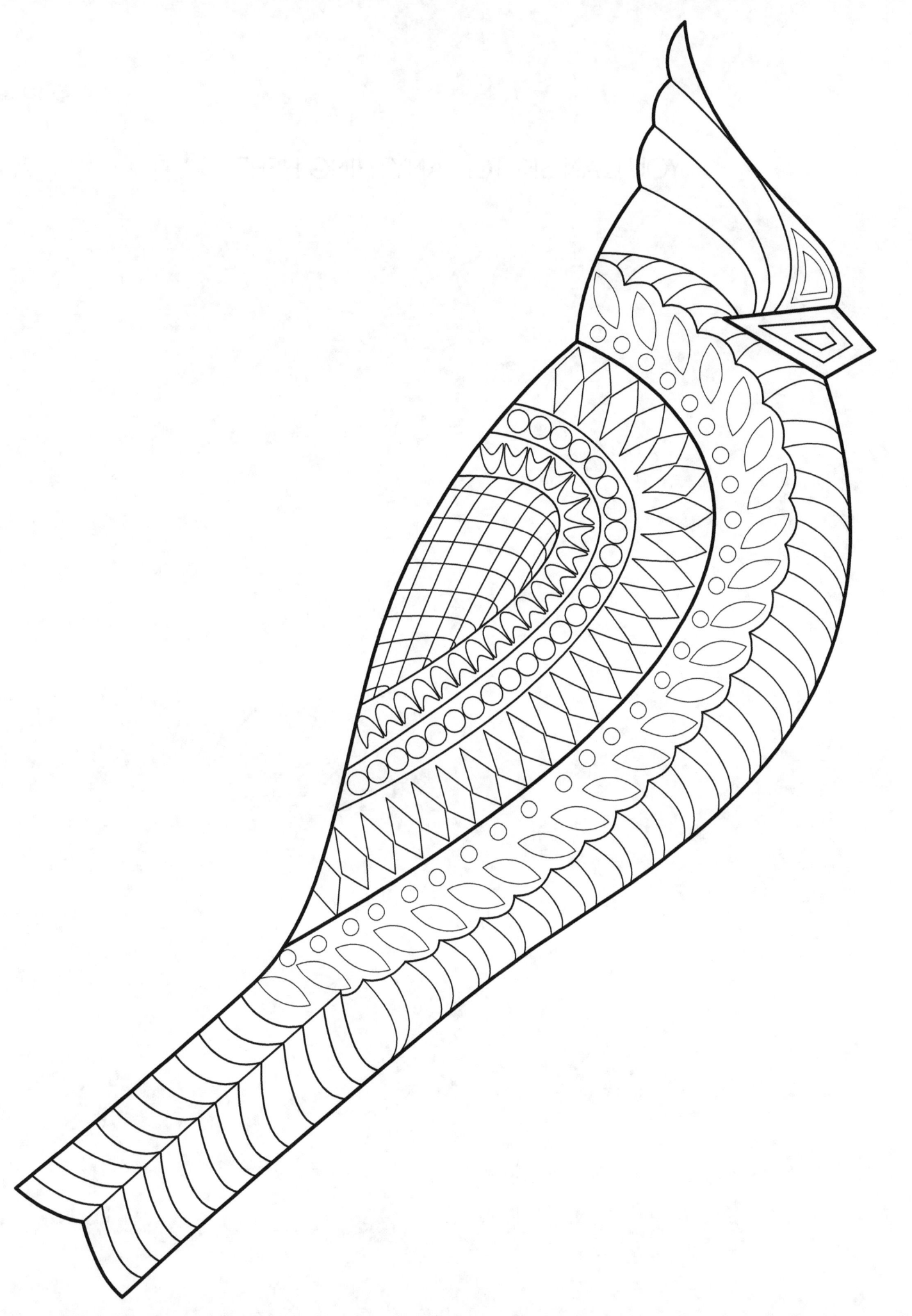

YOU CAN SKETCH ANYTHING HERE

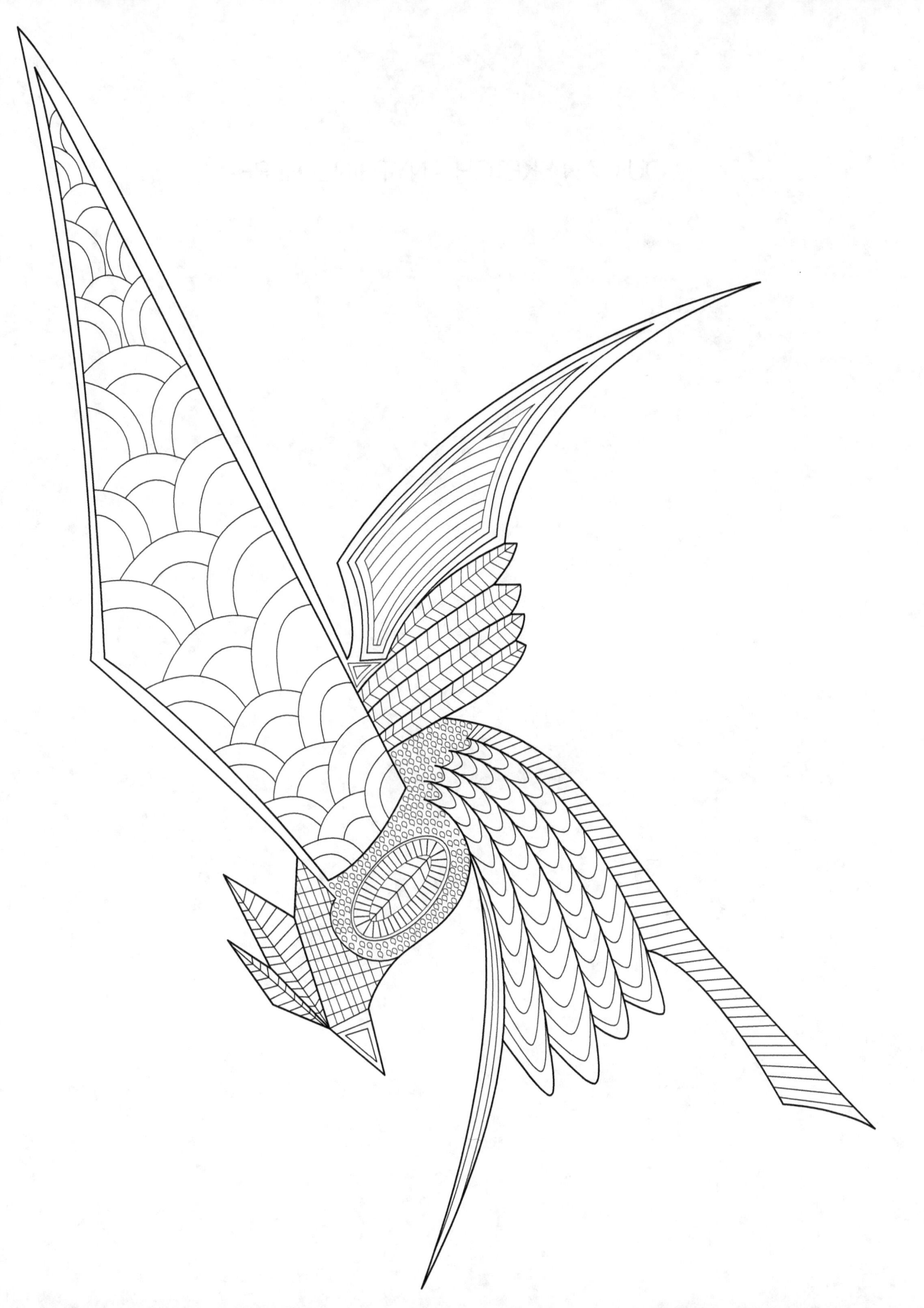

YOU CAN SKETCH ANYTHING HERE

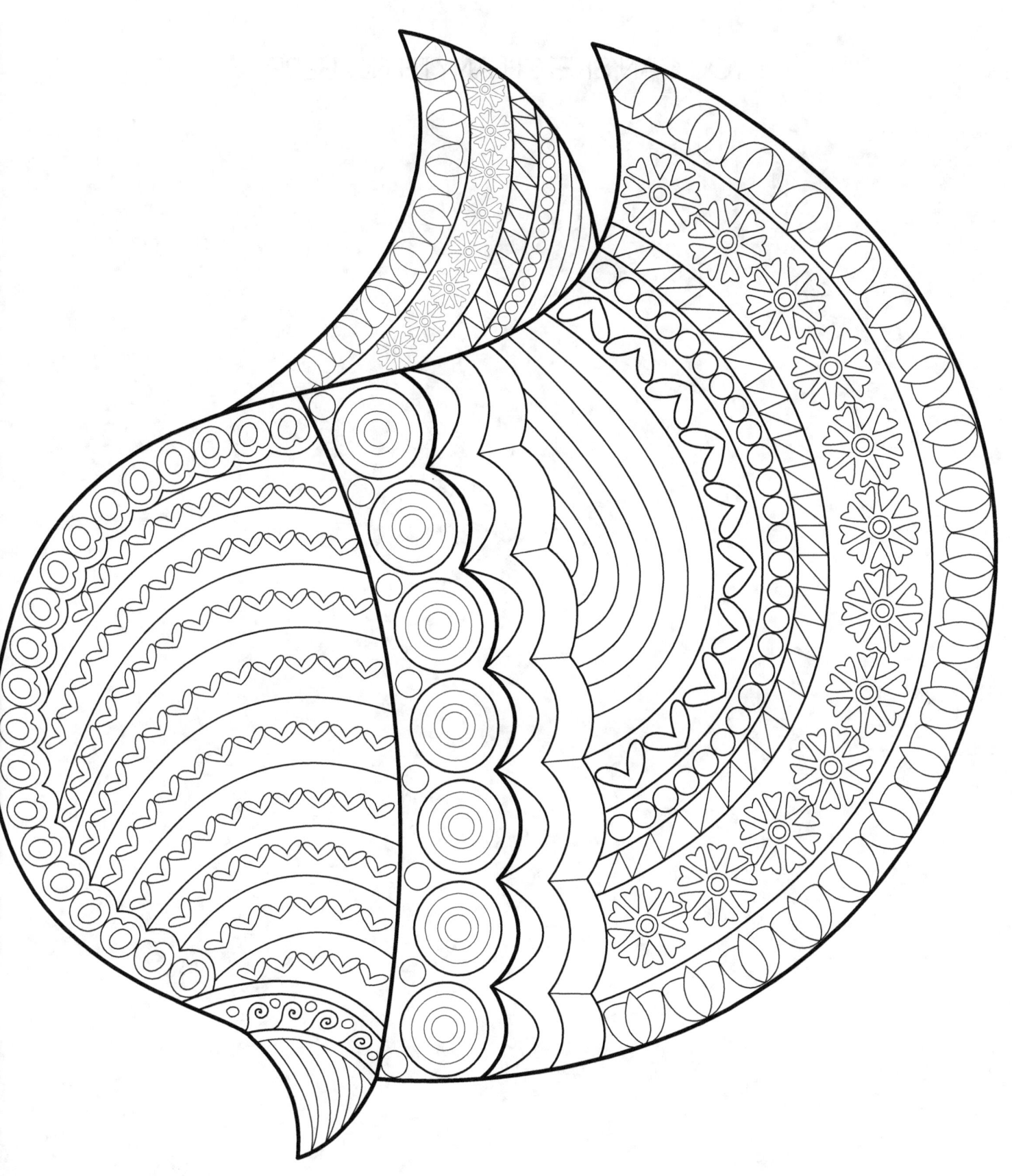

YOU CAN SKETCH ANYTHING HERE

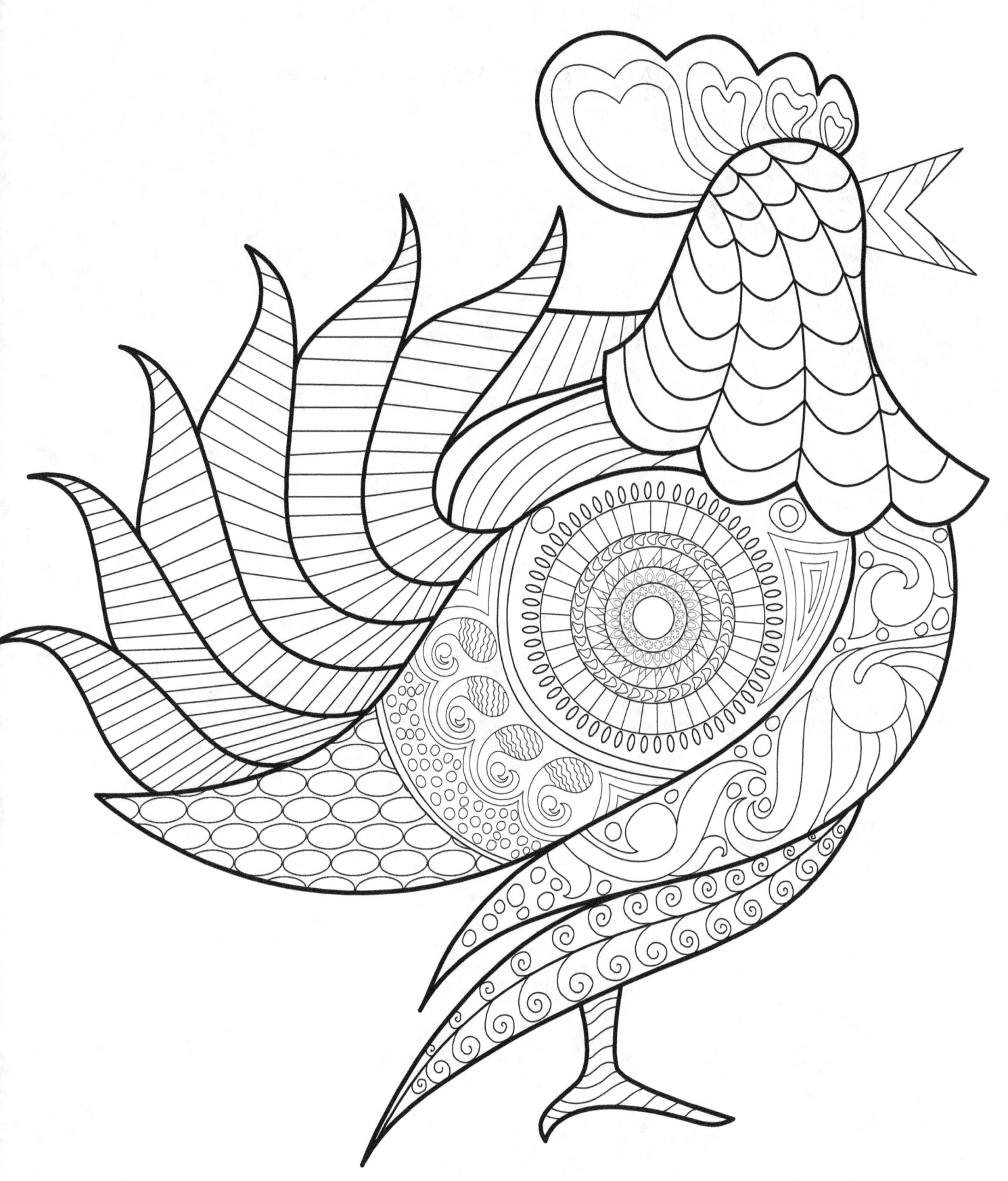

YOU CAN SKETCH ANYTHING HERE

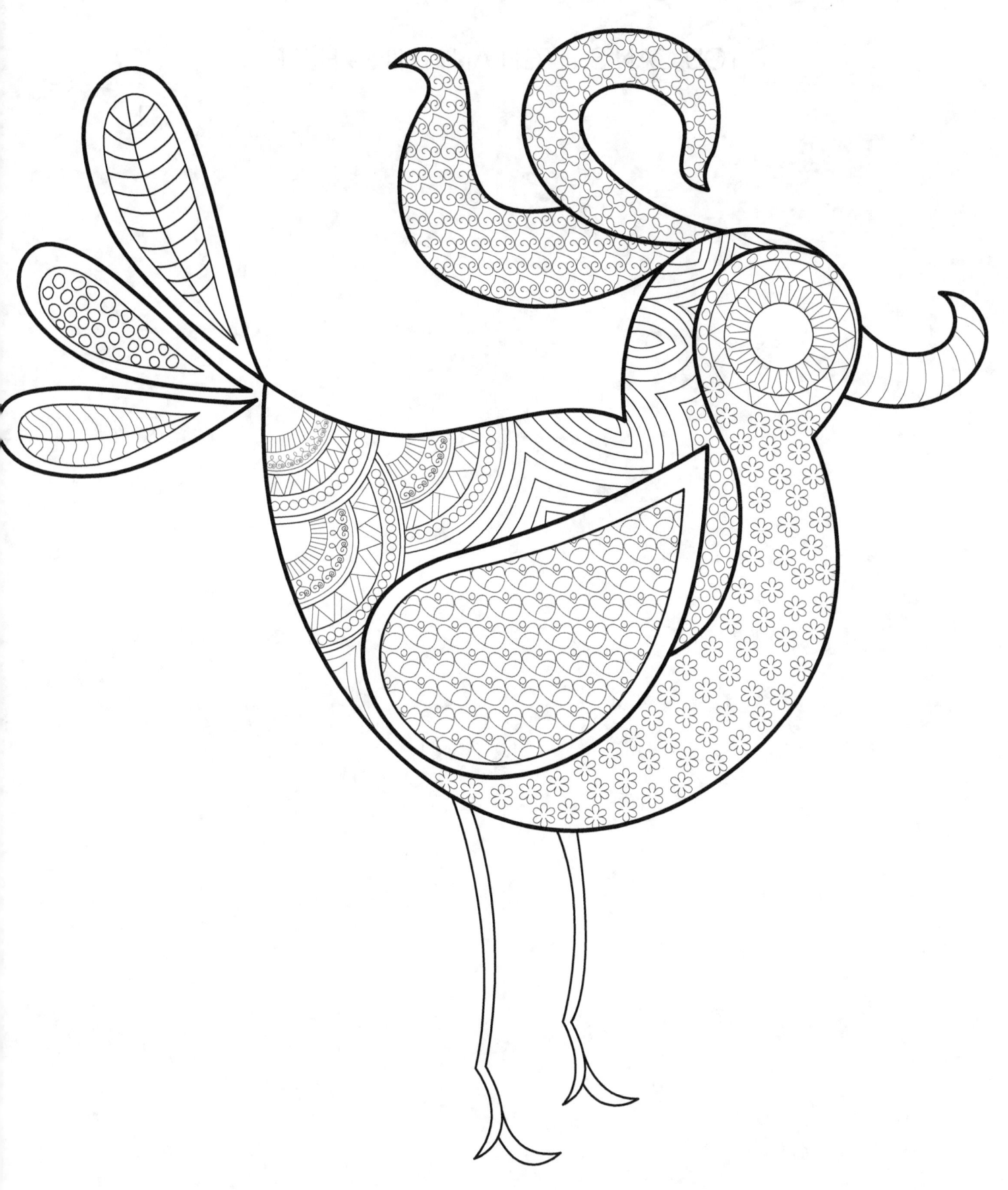

YOU CAN SKETCH ANYTHING HERE

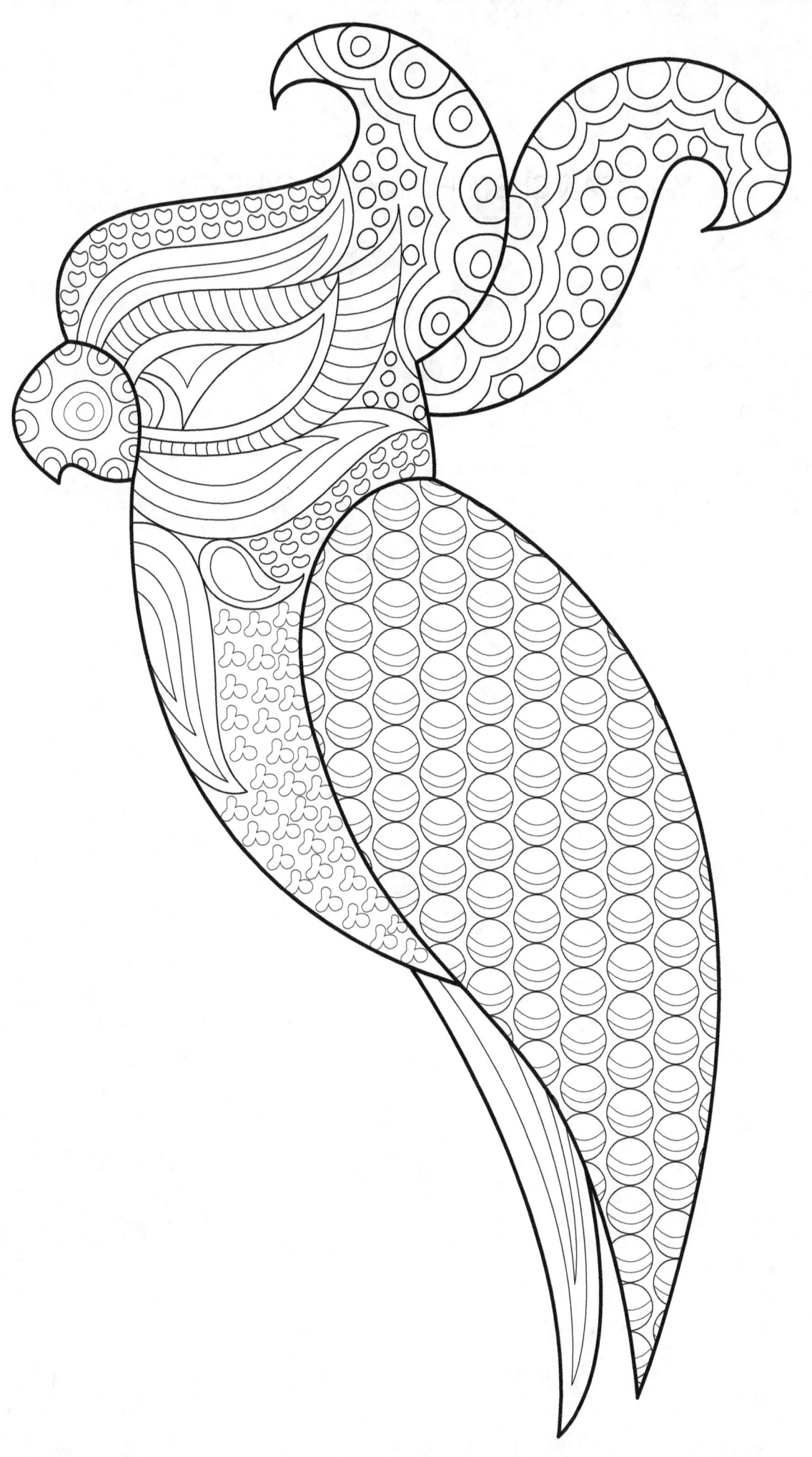

YOU CAN SKETCH ANYTHING HERE

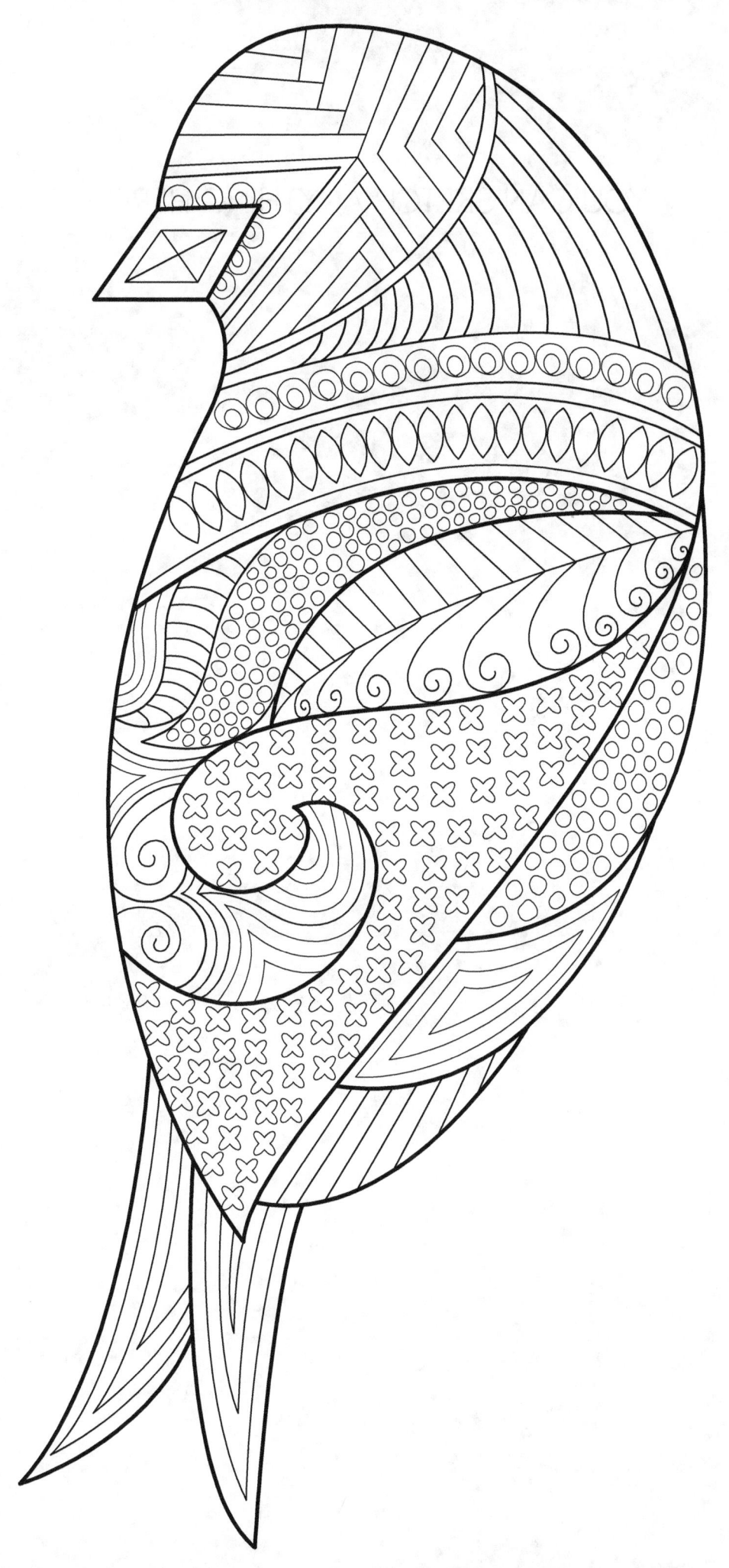

YOU CAN SKETCH ANYTHING HERE

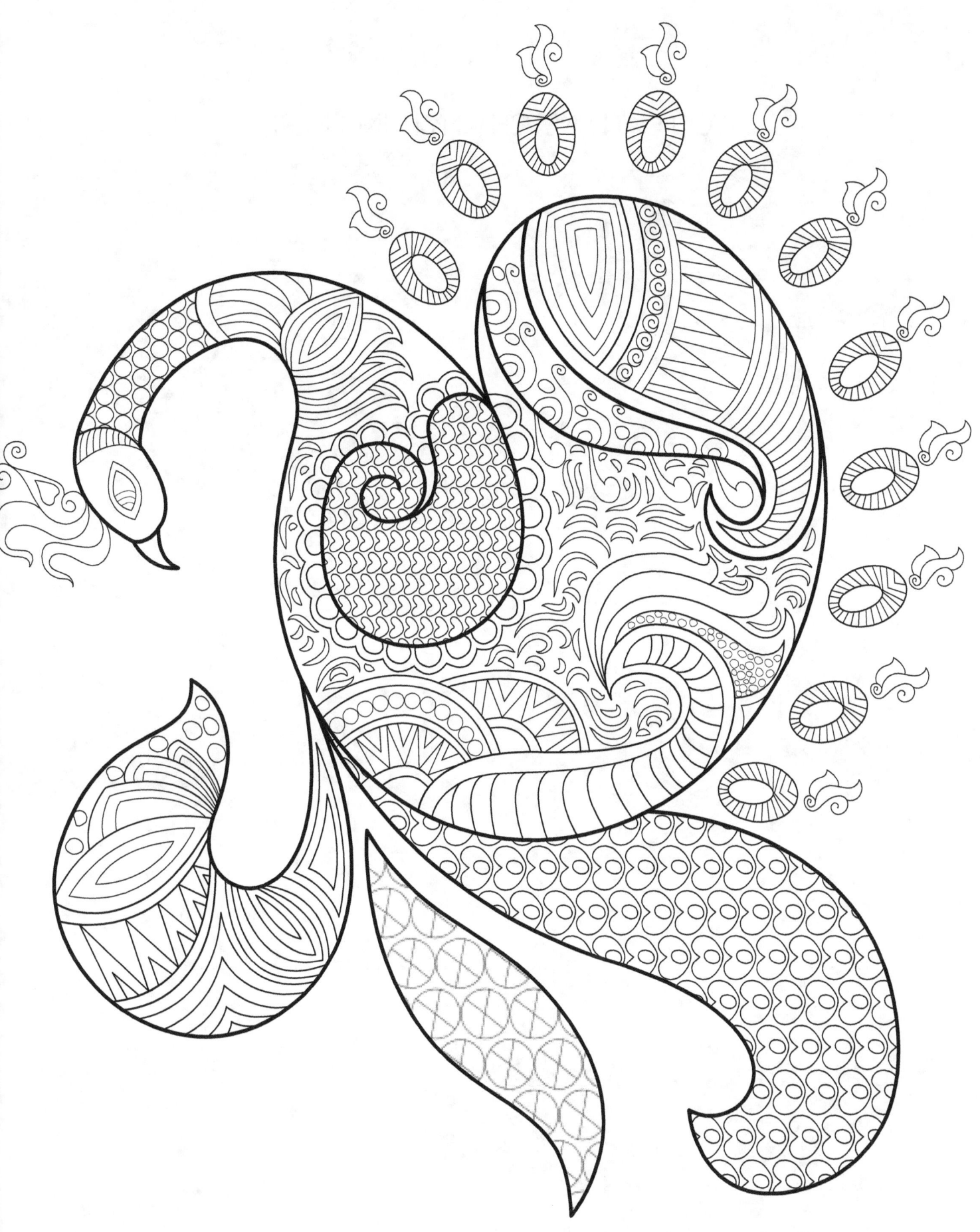

YOU CAN SKETCH ANYTHING HERE

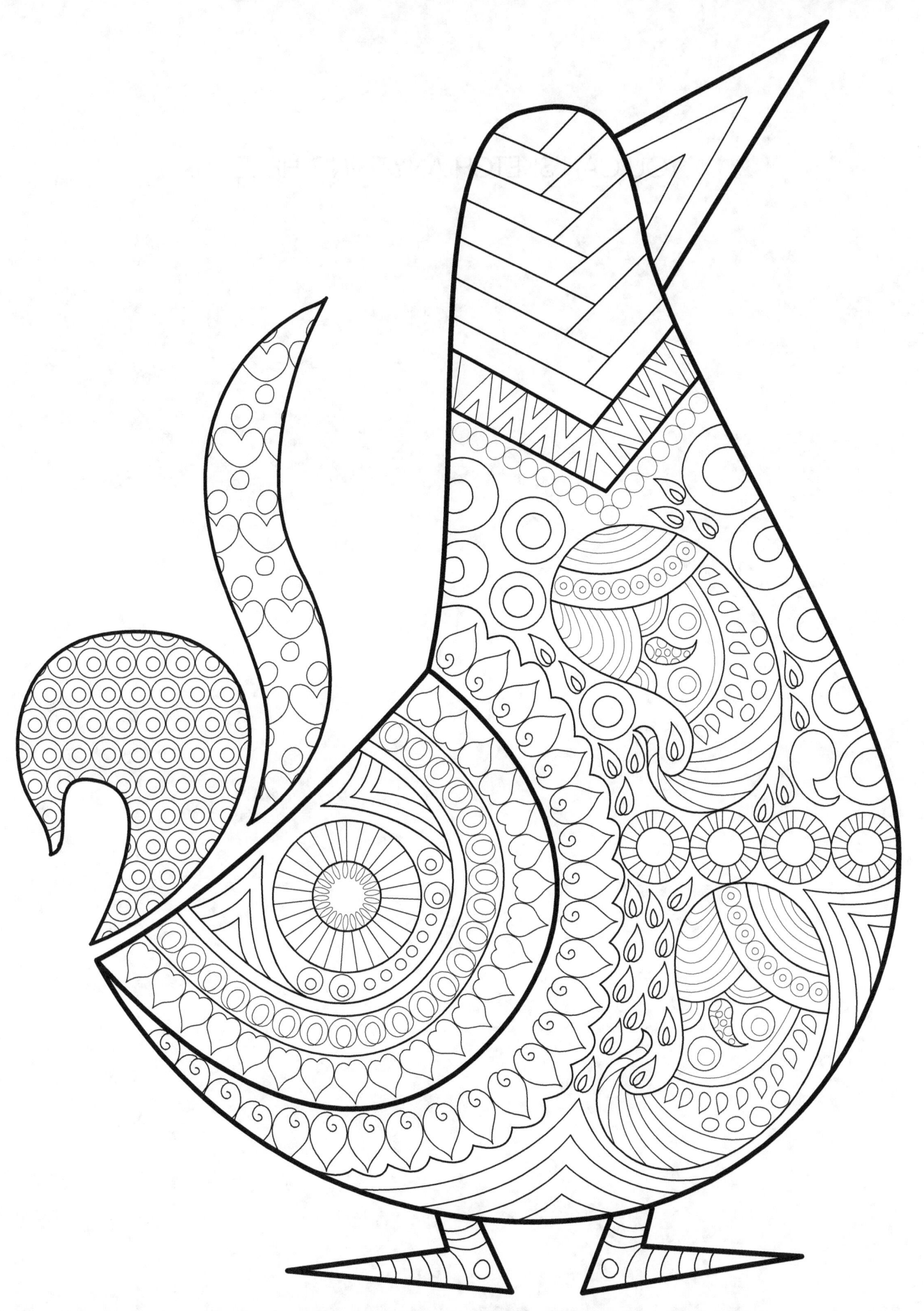

YOU CAN SKETCH ANYTHING HERE

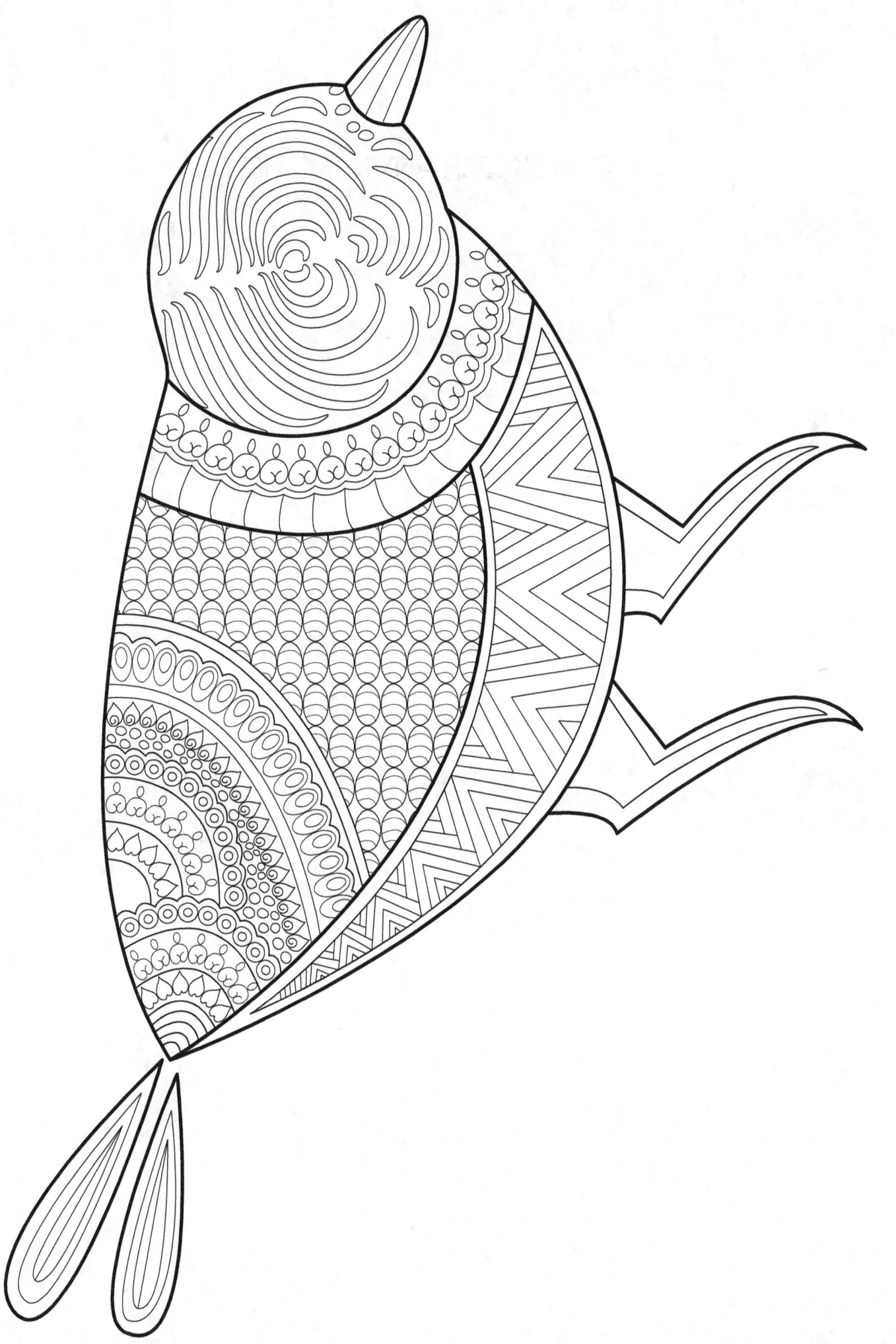

YOU CAN SKETCH ANYTHING HERE

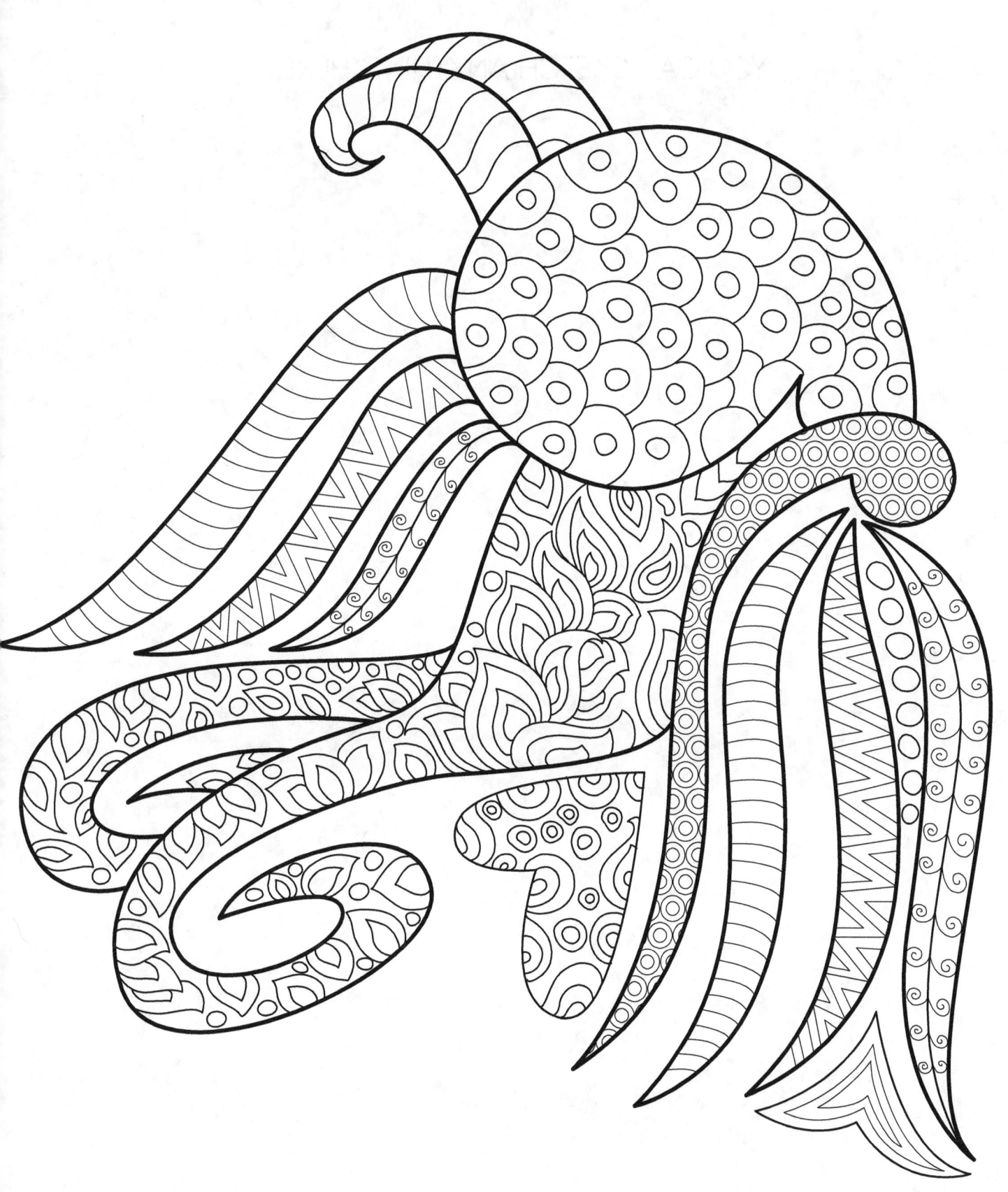

YOU CAN SKETCH ANYTHING HERE

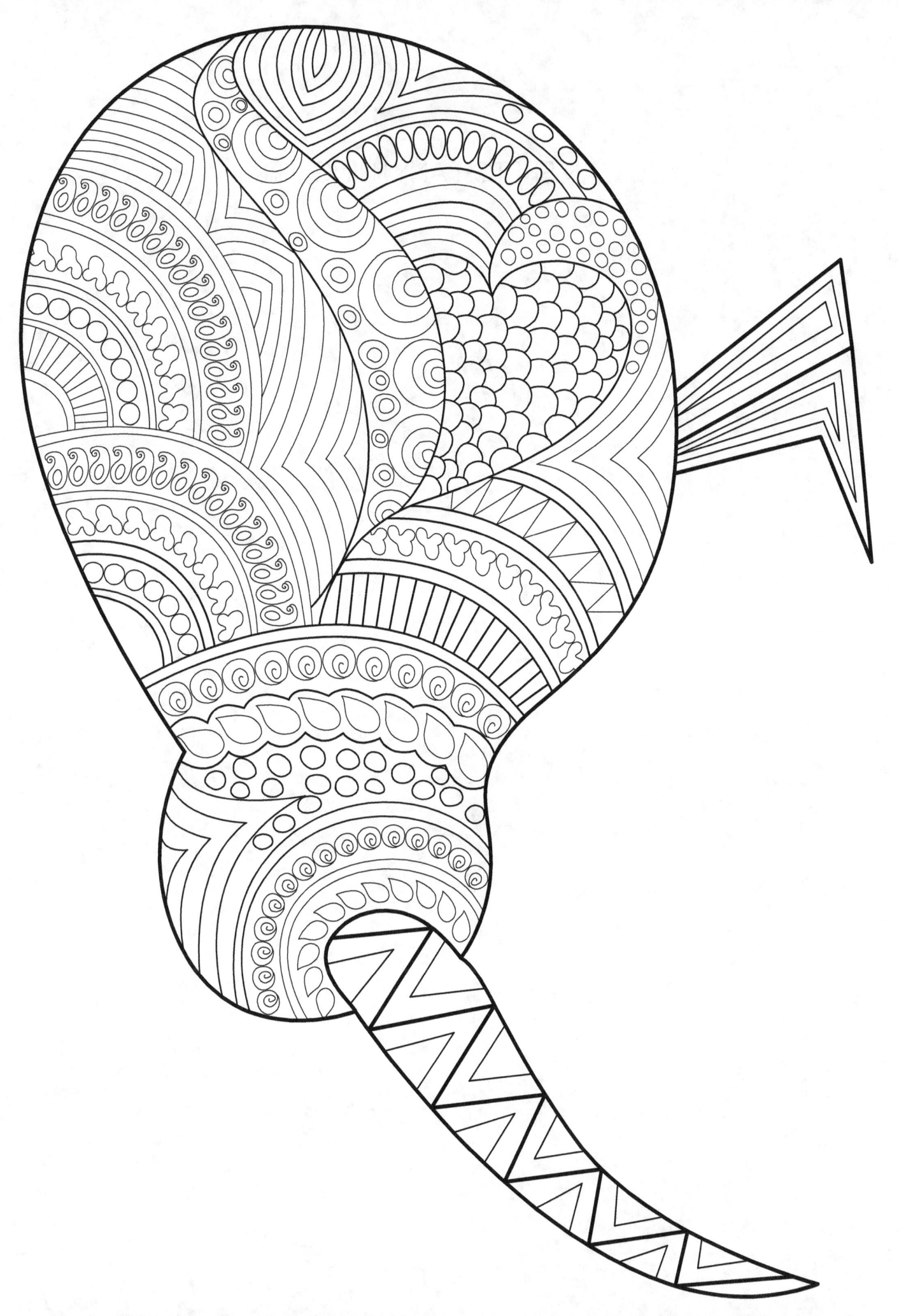

YOU CAN SKETCH ANYTHING HERE

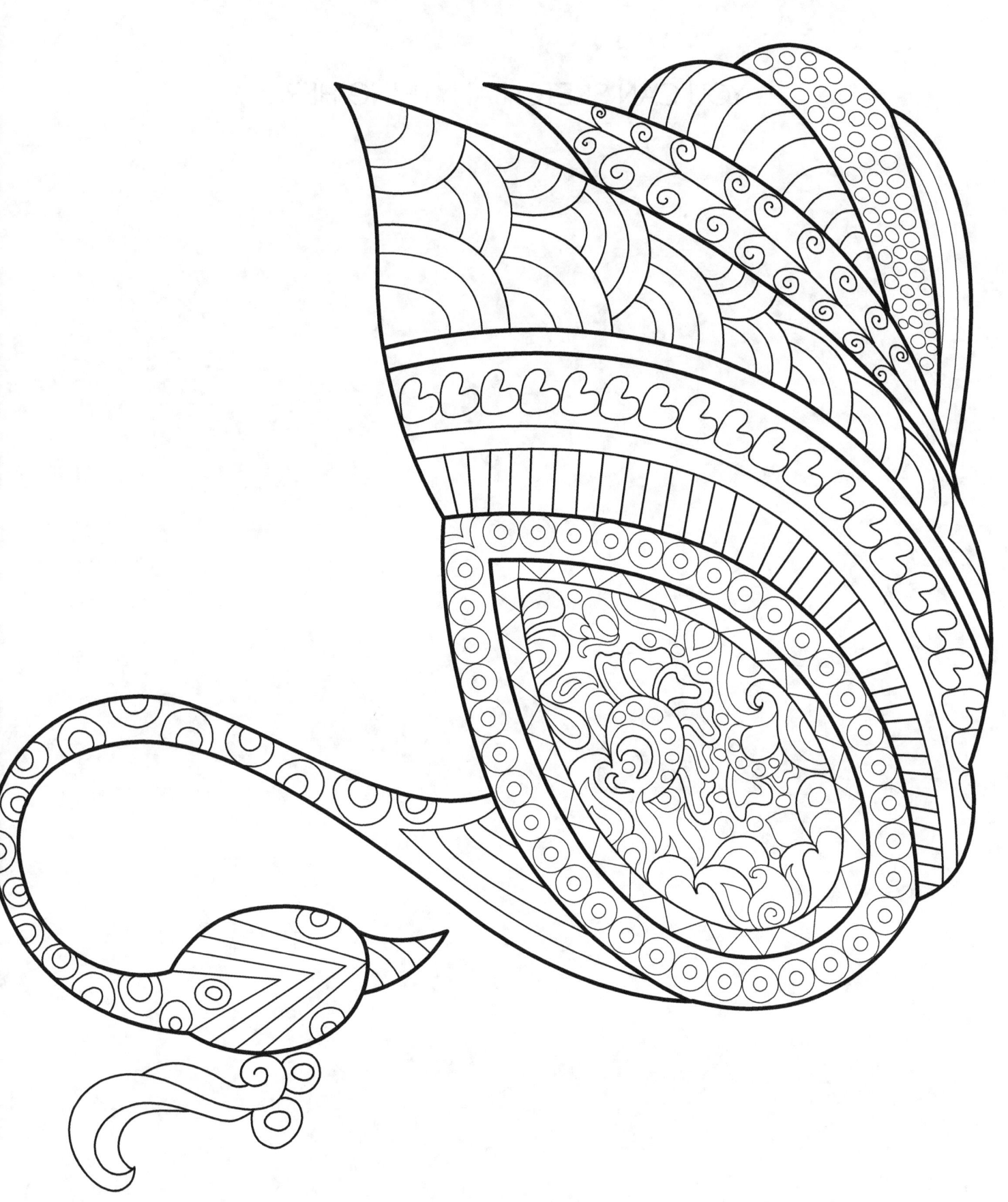

YOU CAN SKETCH ANYTHING HERE

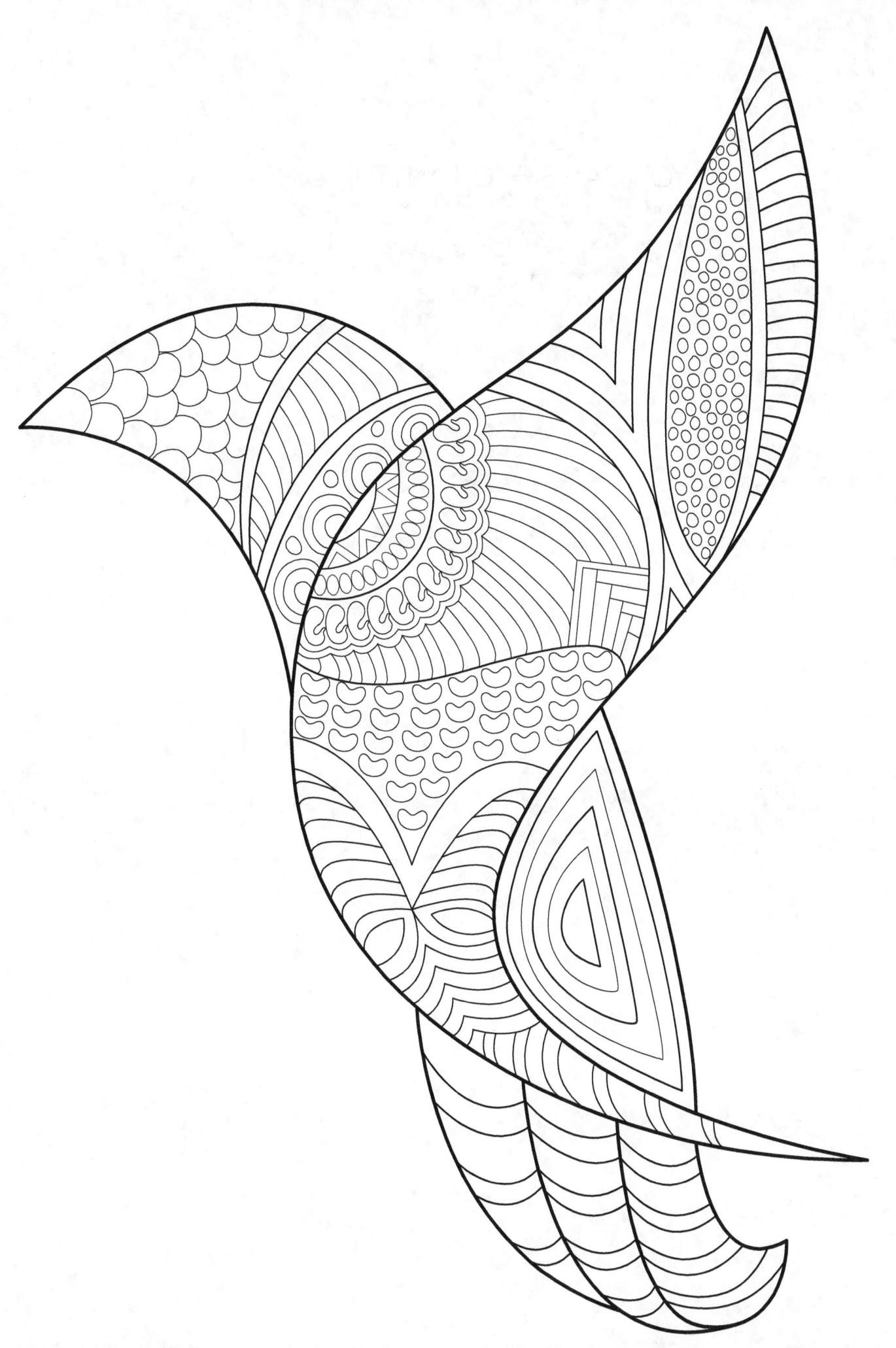

YOU CAN SKETCH ANYTHING HERE

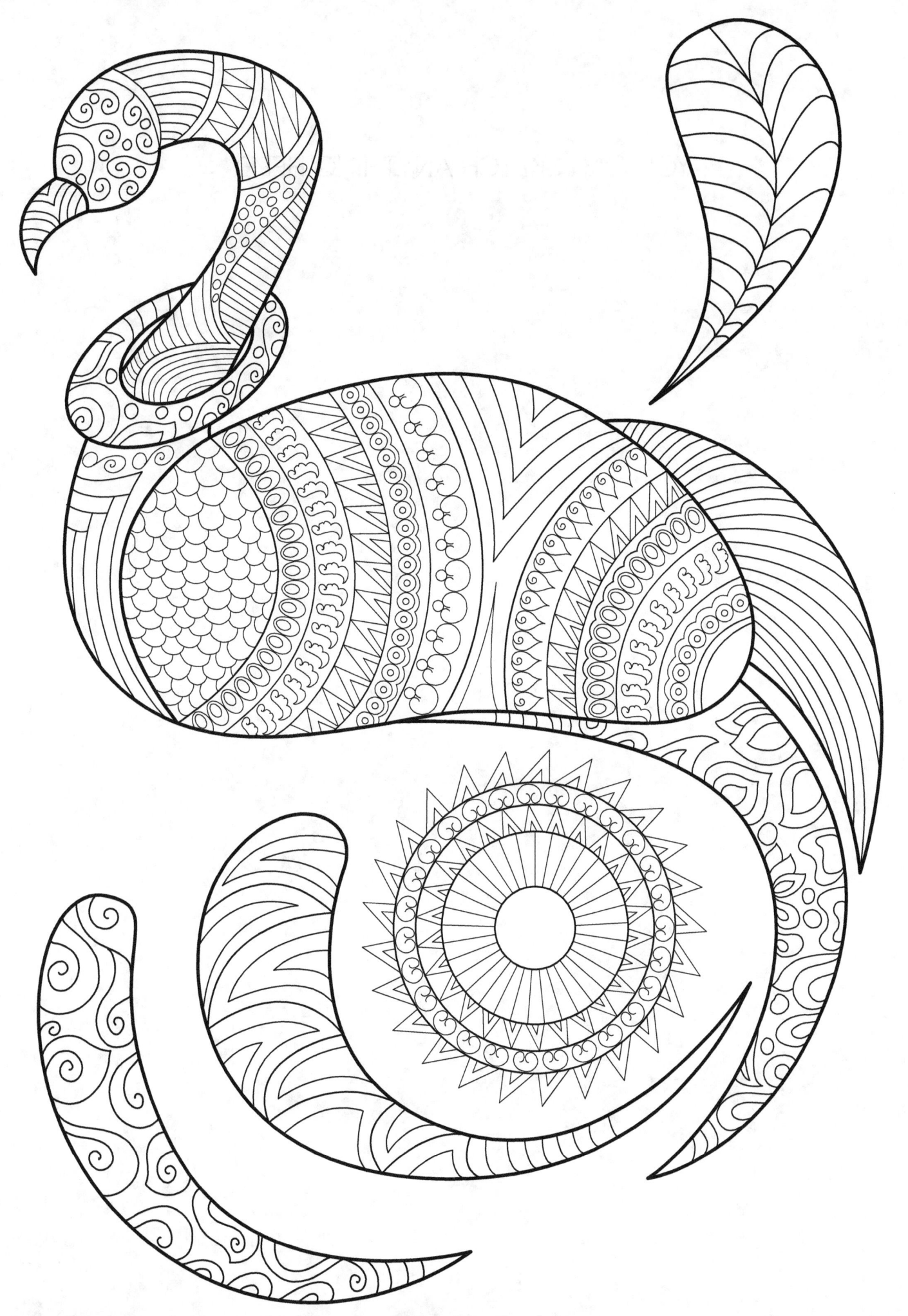

YOU CAN SKETCH ANYTHING HERE

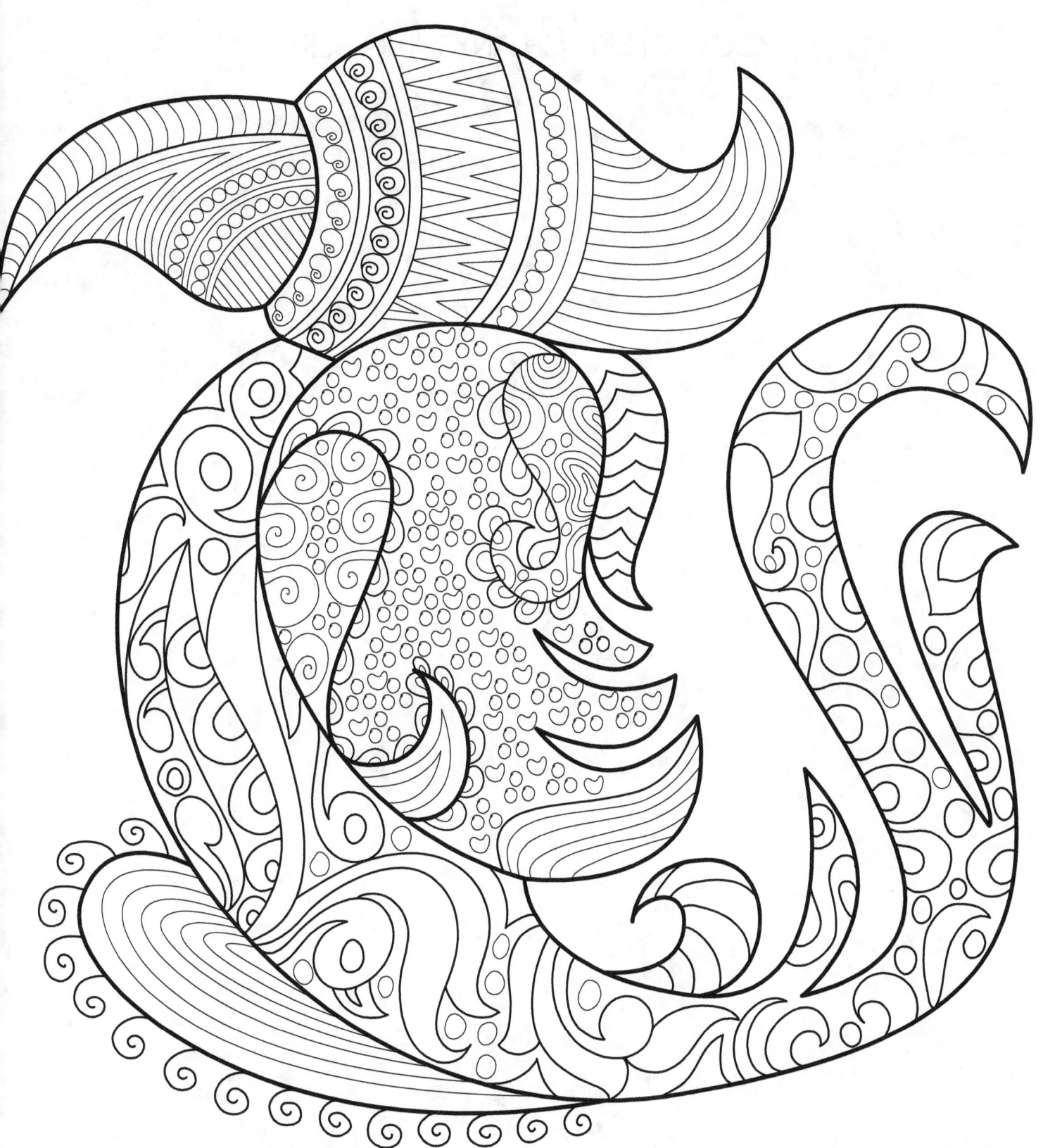

YOU CAN SKETCH ANYTHING HERE

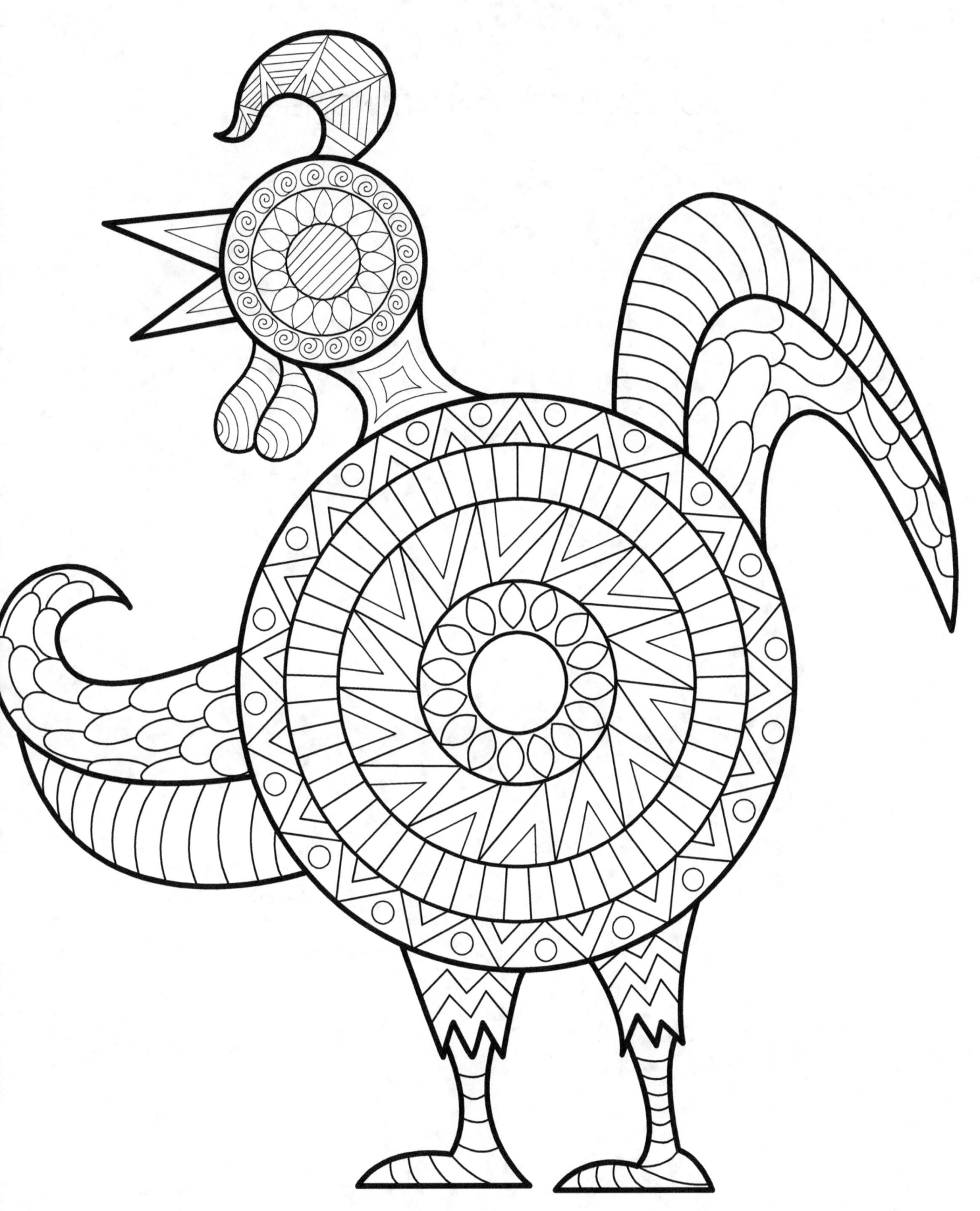

YOU CAN SKETCH ANYTHING HERE

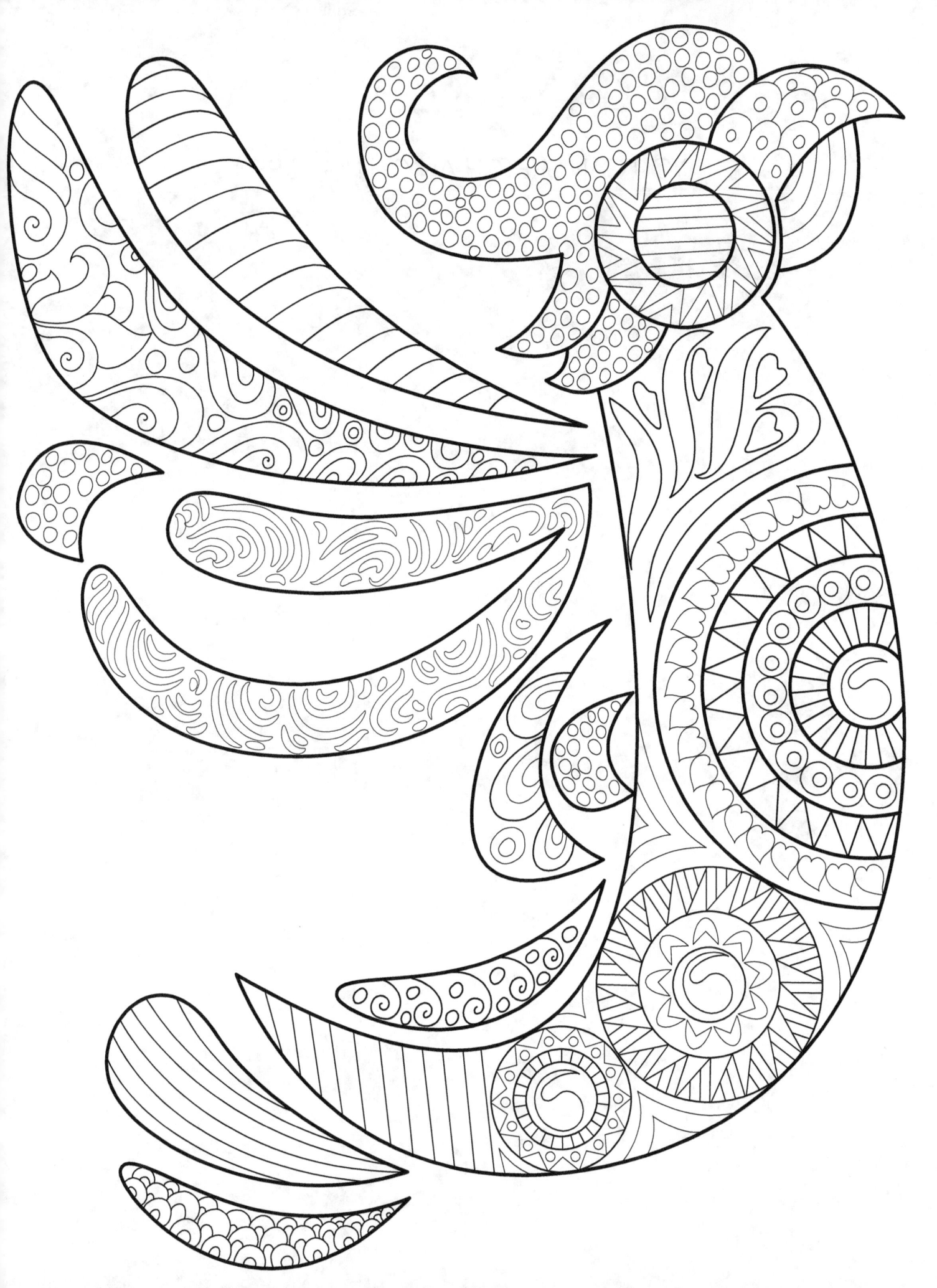

YOU CAN SKETCH ANYTHING HERE

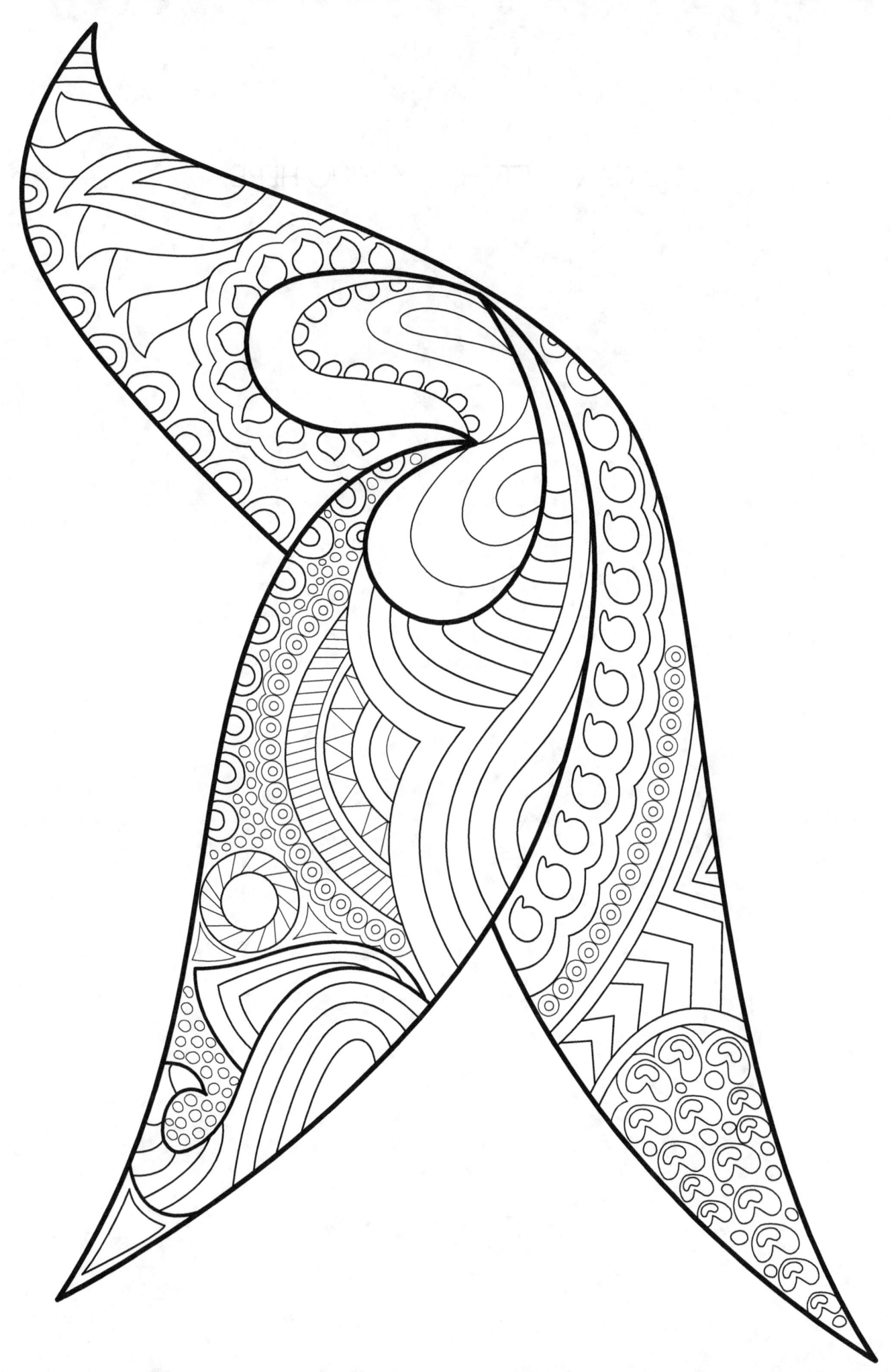

YOU CAN SKETCH ANYTHING HERE

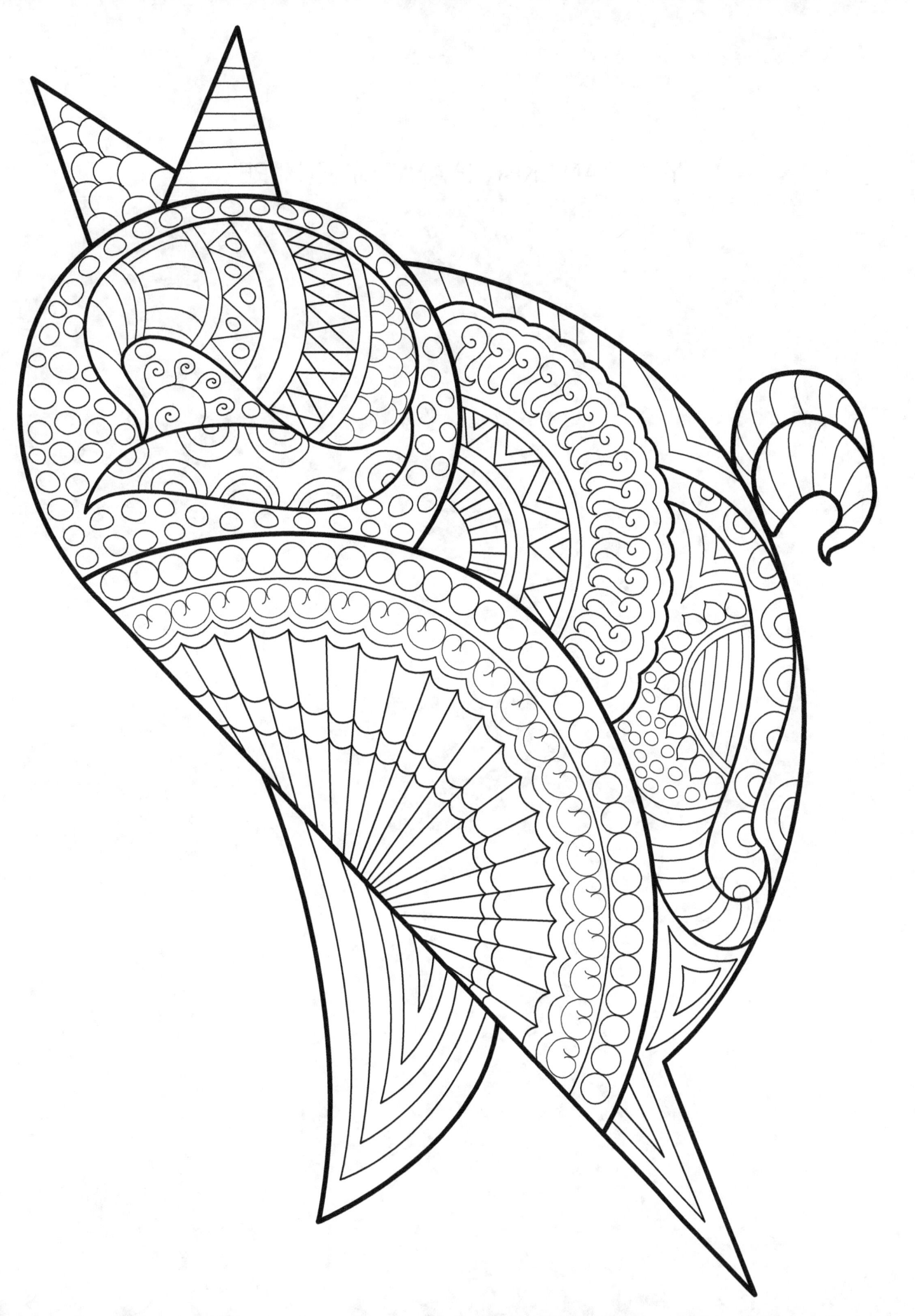

YOU CAN SKETCH ANYTHING HERE

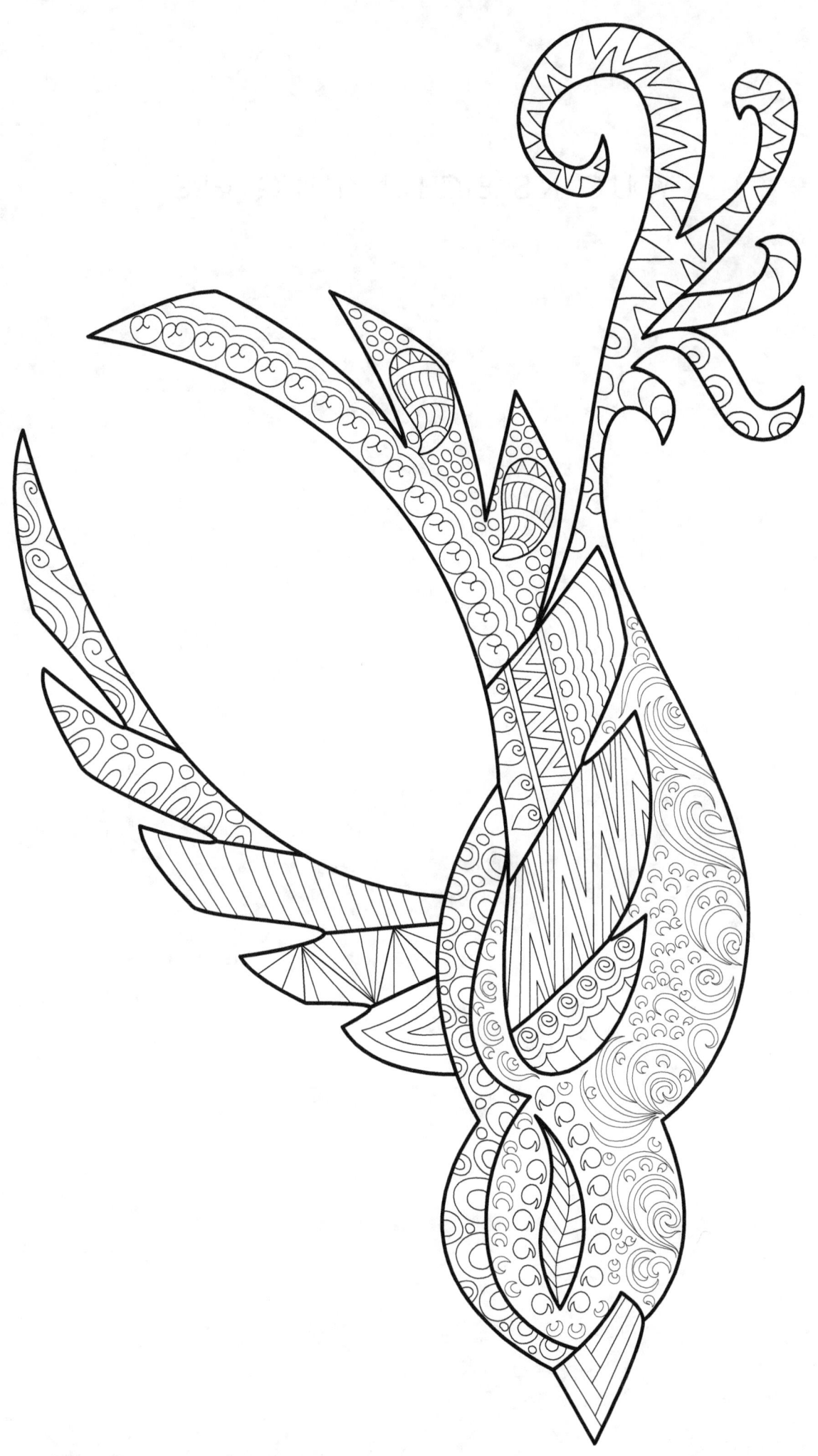

YOU CAN SKETCH ANYTHING HERE

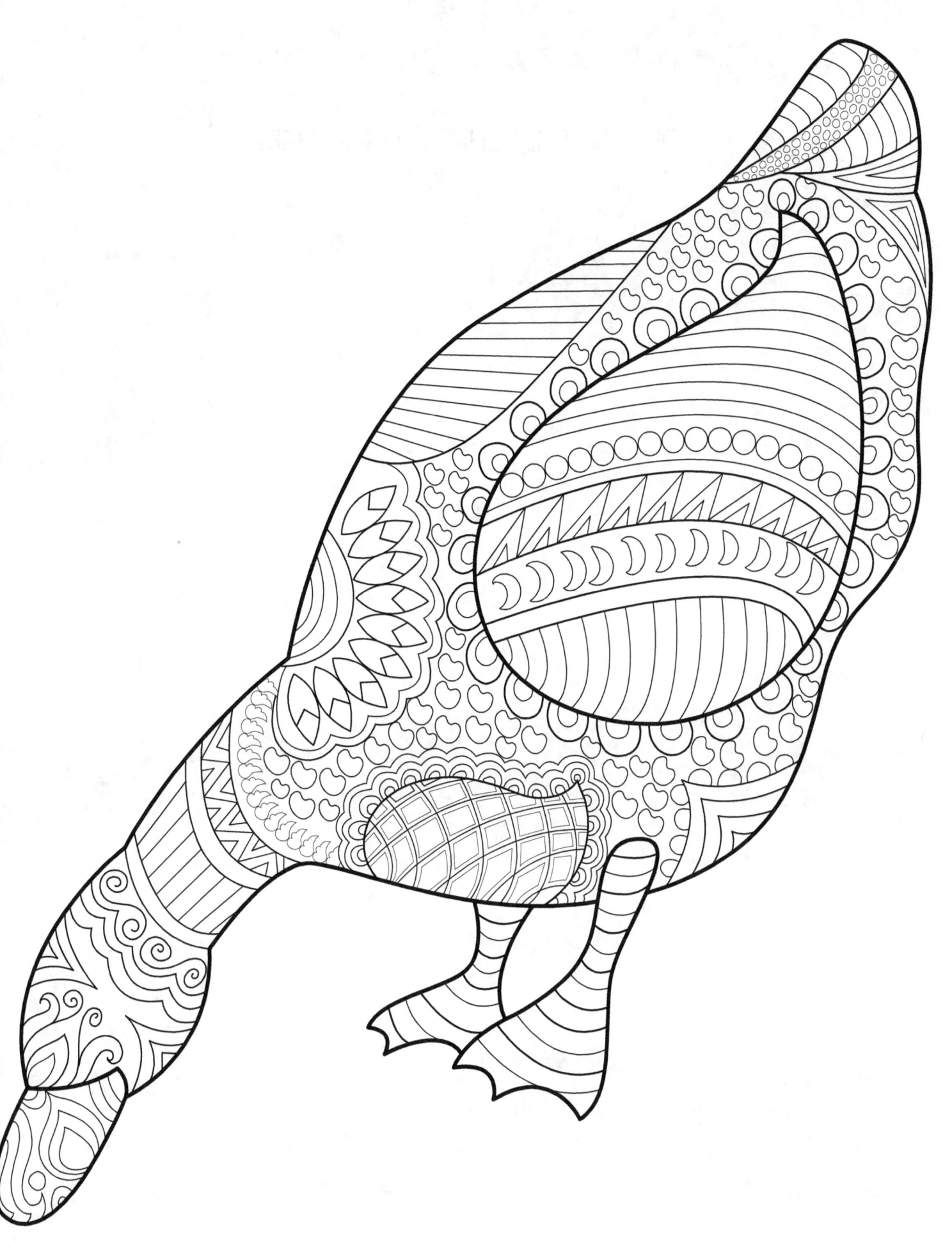

YOU CAN SKETCH ANYTHING HERE

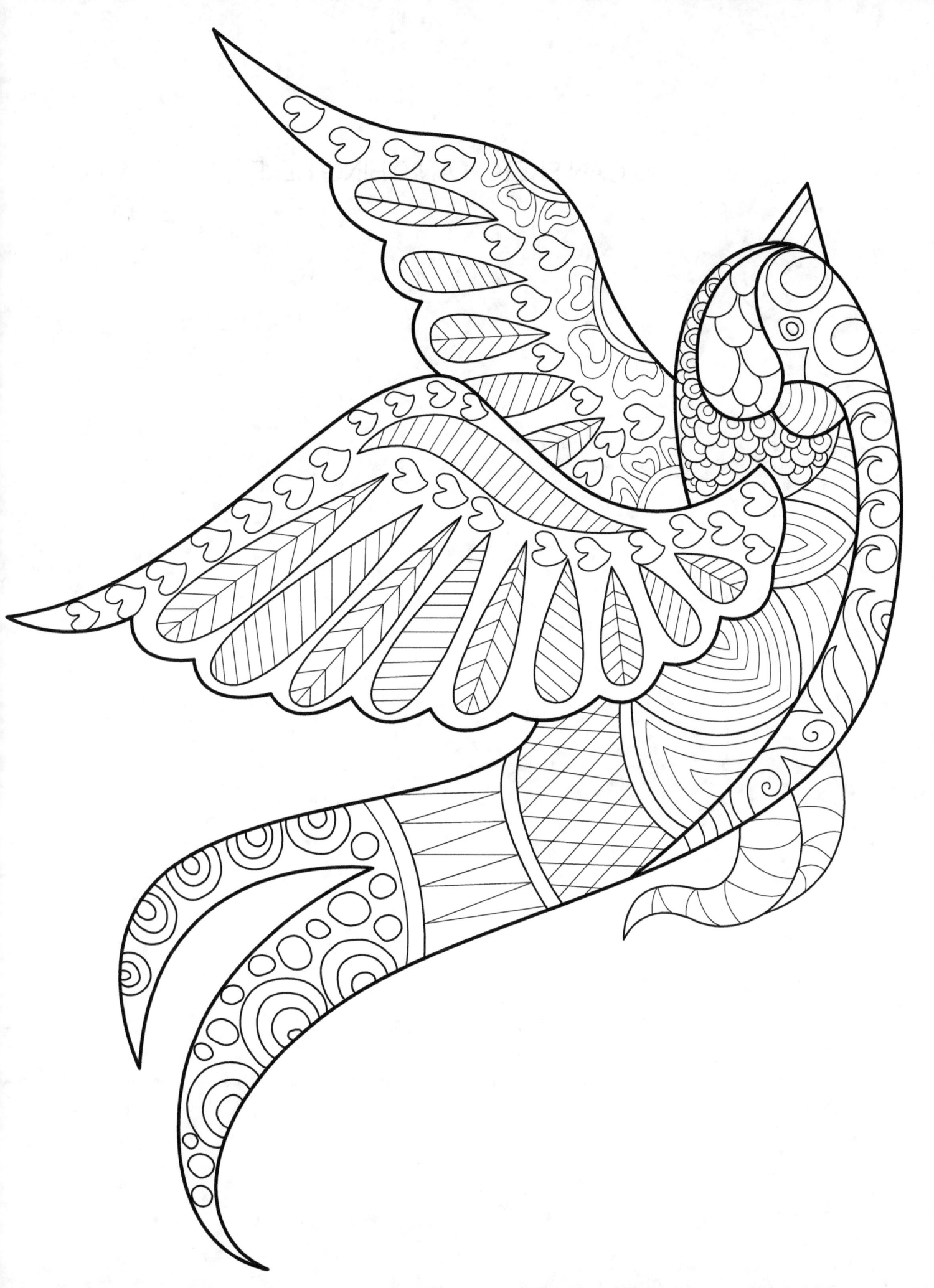

YOU CAN SKETCH ANYTHING HERE

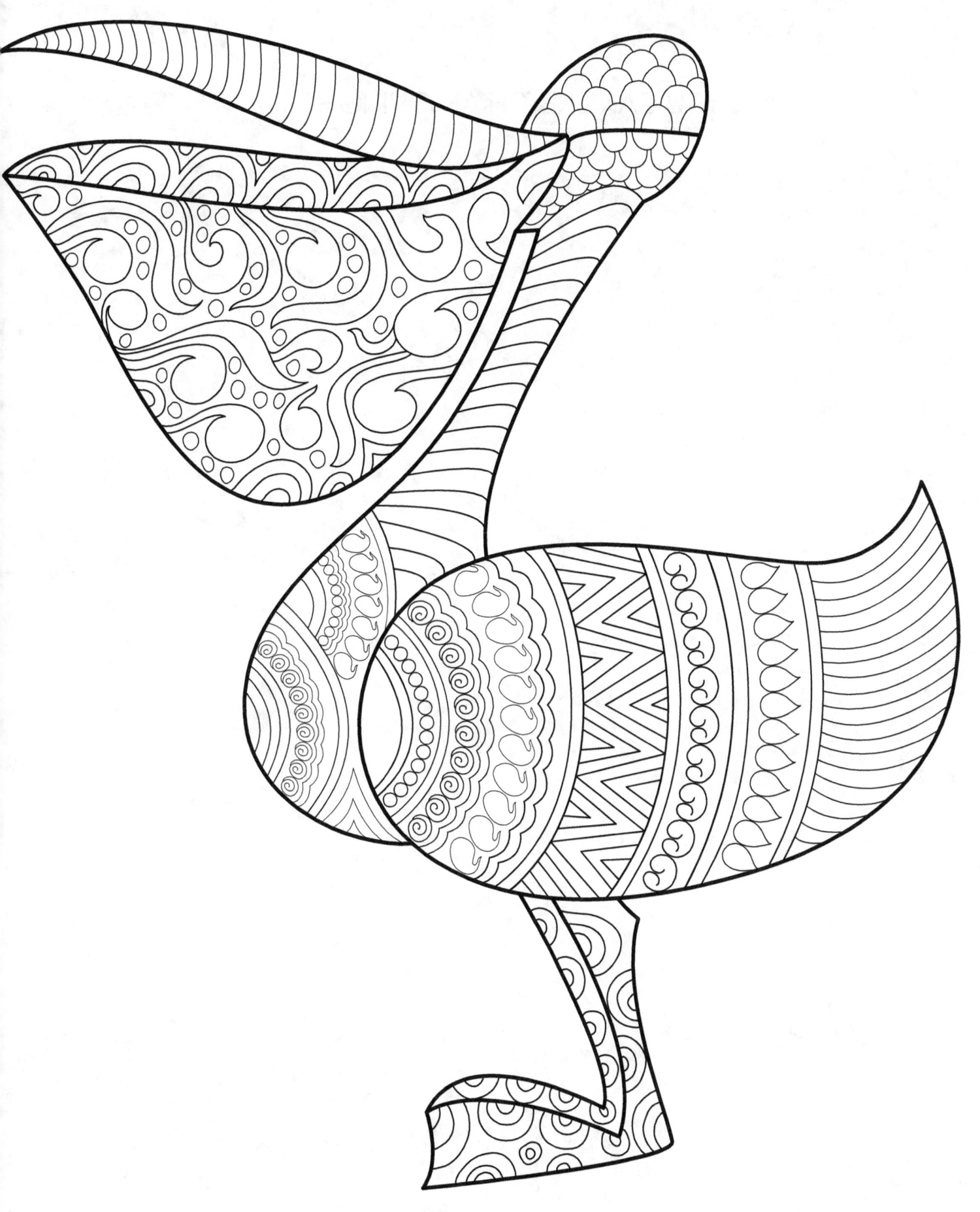

YOU CAN SKETCH ANYTHING HERE

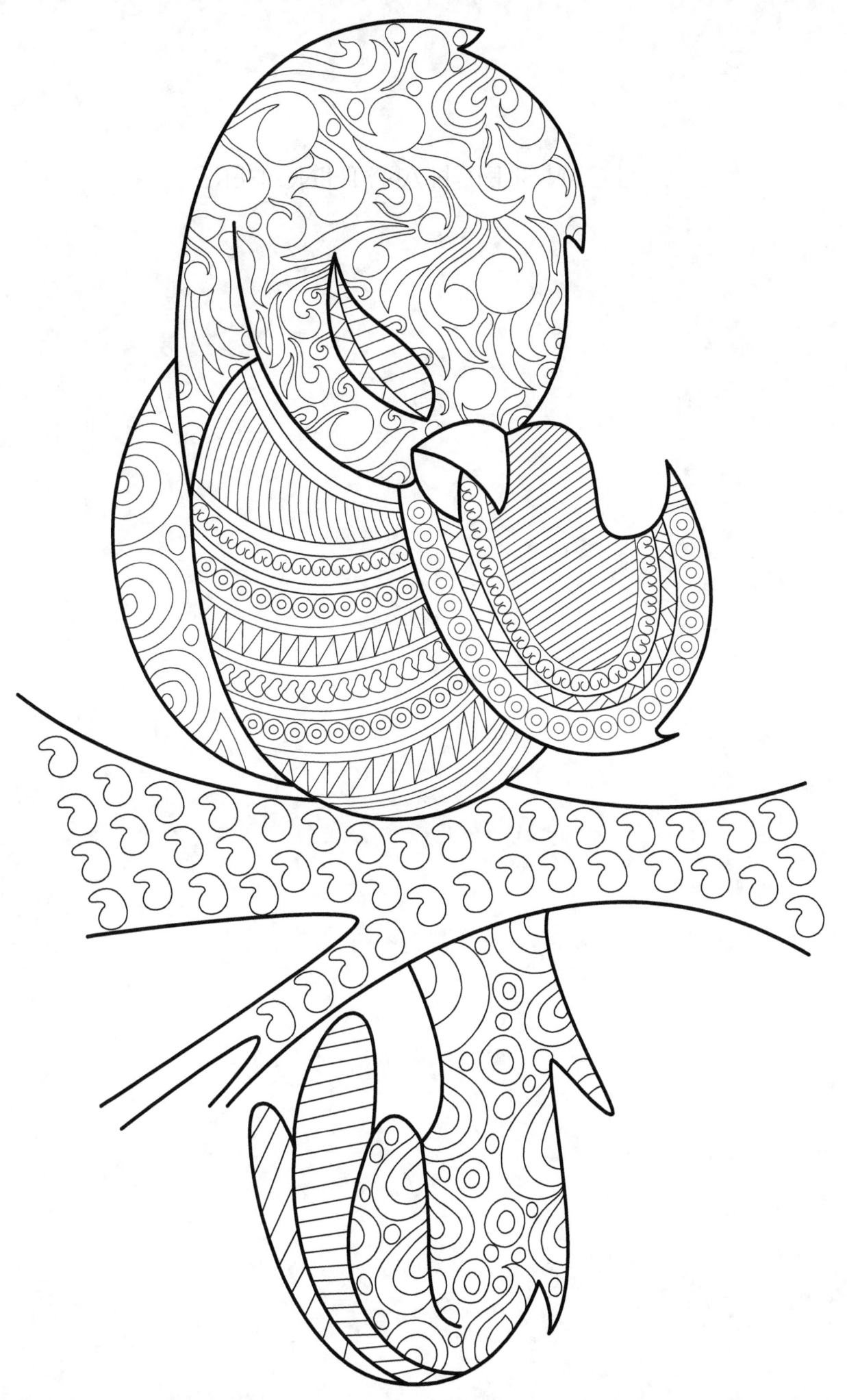

YOU CAN SKETCH ANYTHING HERE

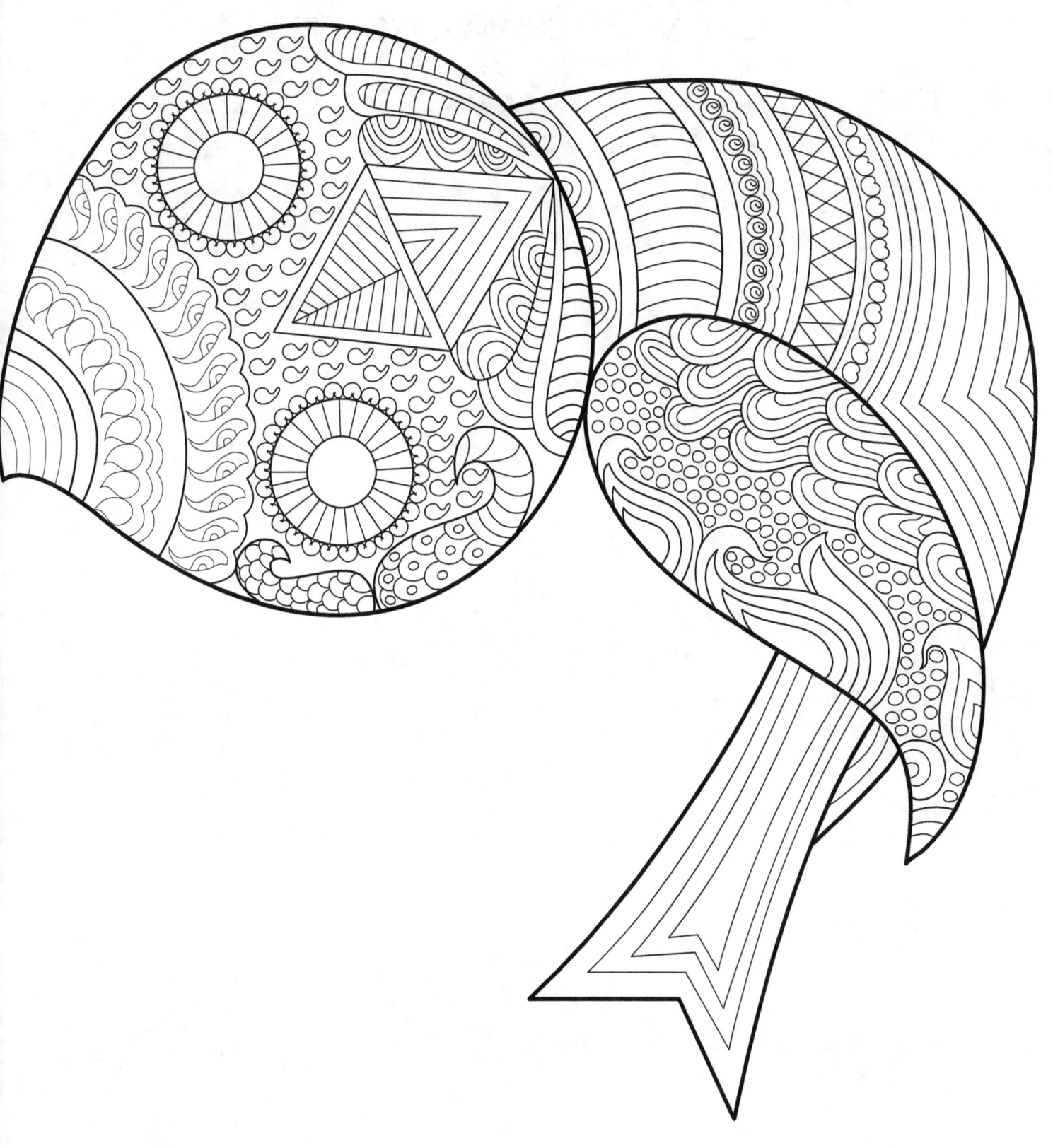

YOU CAN SKETCH ANYTHING HERE

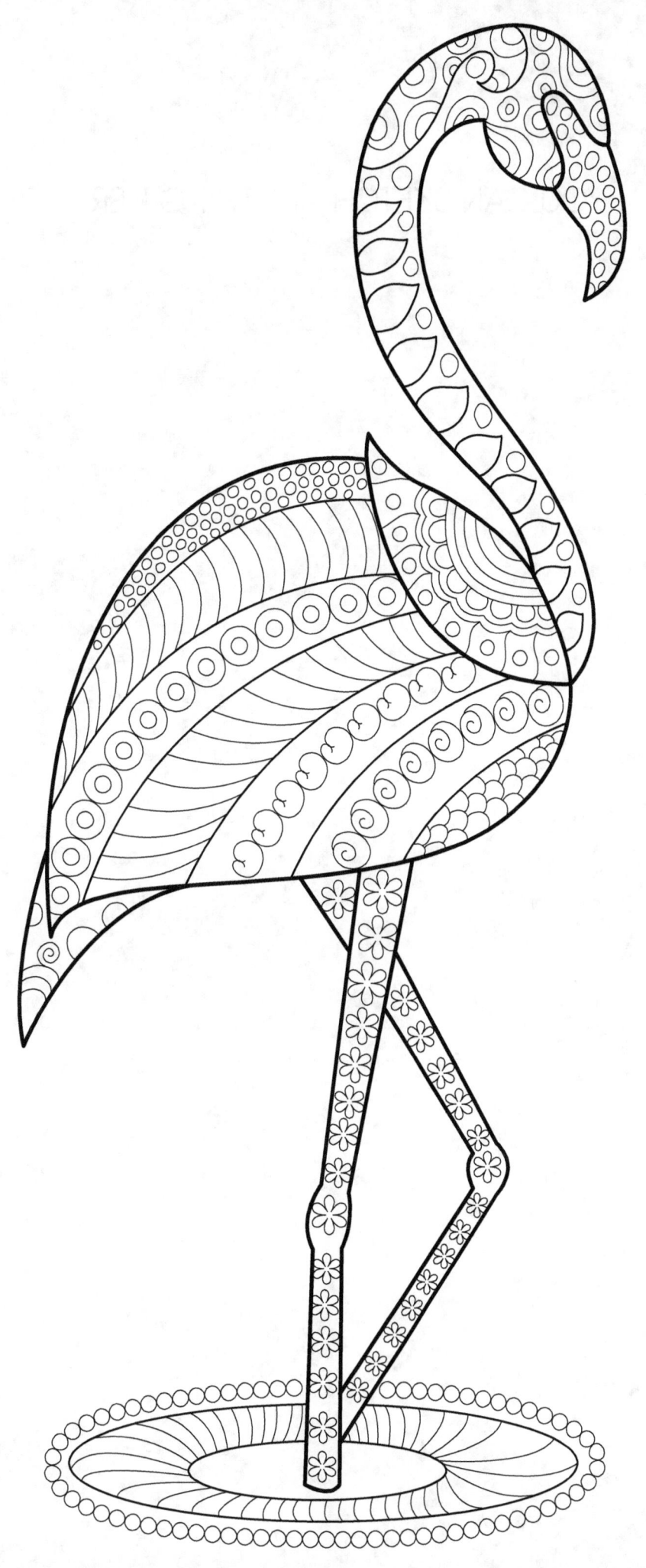

YOU CAN SKETCH ANYTHING HERE

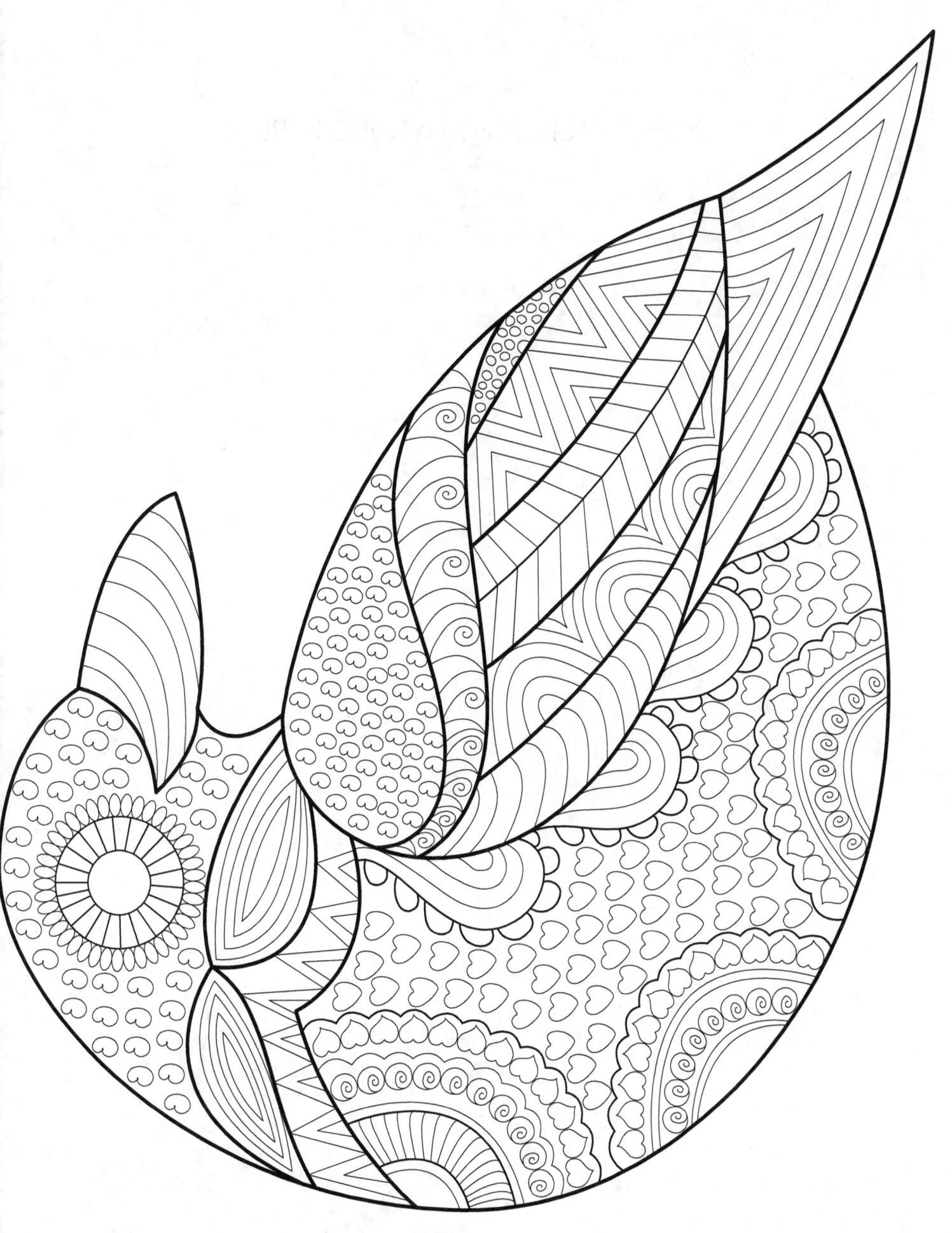

YOU CAN SKETCH ANYTHING HERE

Bored? Sovle this Maze

Start Here

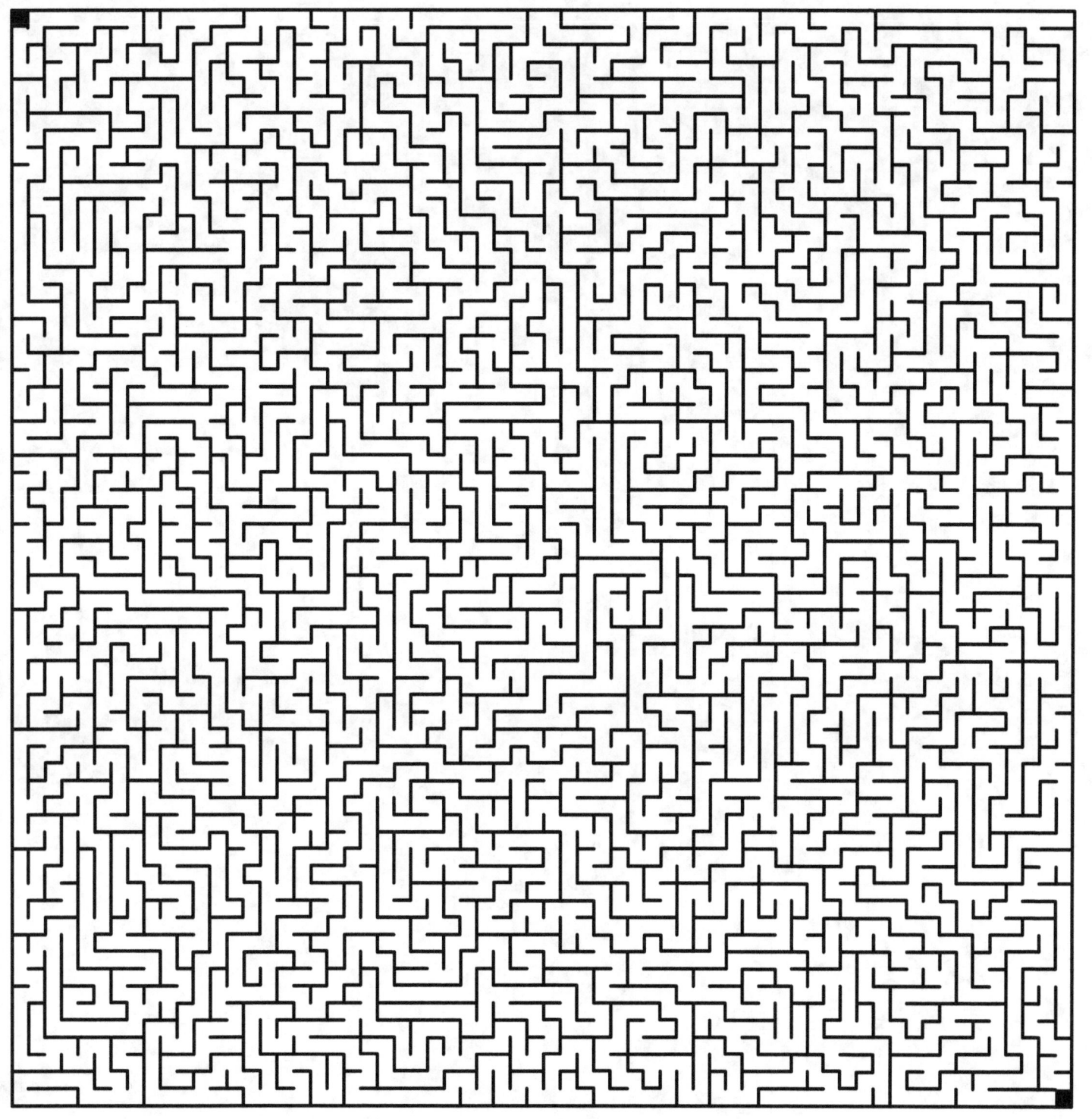

End Here